Jesus Among the Homeless

The House of Prisca and Aquila

Our mission at the House of Prisca and Aquila is to produce quality books that expound accurately the word of God to empower women and men to minister together in a multicultural church. Our writers have a positive view of the Bible as God's revelation that affects both thoughts and words, so it is plenary, historically accurate, and consistent in itself, fully reliable, and authoritative as God's revelation. Because God is true, God's revelation is true, inclusive to men and women, and speaking to a multicultural church, wherein all the diversity of the church is represented within the parameters of egalitarianism and inerrancy.

The word of God is what we are expounding, thereby empowering women and men to minister together in all levels of the church and home. The reason we say women and men together is because that is the model of Prisca and Aquila, ministering together to another member of the church—Apollos: "Having heard Apollos, Priscilla and Aquila took him aside and more accurately expounded to him the Way of God" (Acts 18:26). True exposition, like true religion, is by no means boring—it is fascinating. Books that reveal and expound God's true nature "burn within us" as they elucidate the Scripture and apply it to our lives.

This was the experience of the disciples who heard Jesus on the road to Emmaus: "Were not our hearts burning while Jesus was talking to us on the road, while he was opening the scriptures to us?" (Luke 24:32). We are hoping to create the classics of tomorrow, significant and accessible trade and academic books that "burn within us."

Our "house" is like the home to which Prisca and Aquila no doubt brought Apollos as they took him aside. It is like the home in Emmaus where Jesus stopped to break bread and reveal his presence. It is like the house built on the rock of obedience to Jesus (Matt 7:24). Our "house," as a euphemism for our publishing team, is a home where truth is shared and Jesus' Spirit breaks bread with us, nourishing all of us with his bounty of truth.

We are delighted to work together with Wipf and Stock in this series and welcome submissions on a wide variety of topics from an egalitarian, inerrantist global perspective.

For more information, see our Web site:

https://sites.google.com/site/houseofpriscaandaquila/.

Jesus Among the Homeless

Successful Strategies of Christian Ministers
to the Marginalized

Written and edited by
WILMA FAYE MATHIS

Foreword by
JULIA C. DAVIS

Afterword by
OLGA SOLER

WIPF & STOCK · Eugene, Oregon

JESUS AMONG THE HOMELESS
Successful Strategies of Christian Ministers to the Marginalized

House of Prisca and Aquila Series

Wipf & Stock
An Imprint of Wipf and Stock Publishers
199 W. 8th Ave., Suite 3
Eugene, OR 97401

www.wipfandstock.com

PAPERBACK ISBN: 978-1-6667-5888-7
HARDCOVER ISBN: 978-1-6667-5889-4
EBOOK ISBN: 978-1-6667-5890-0

01/23/23

By the Same Authors

Julia C. Davis

Empowering English Language Learners, contributing author.

Specialist Fourth Class John Joseph DeFazio: Advocating for Disabled American Veterans, contributing author.

An Artistic Tribute to Harriet Tubman, co-editor.

The Commission, contributing author.

Finding a Better Way, contributing author.

The Christian World Liberation Front, contributing author.

Jeanne C. DeFazio

Creative Ways to Build Christian Community, co-editor with John P. Lathrop.

How to Have an Attitude of Gratitude on the Night Shift, co-author with Teresa Flowers.

Redeeming the Screens, co-editor with William David Spencer.

Berkeley Street Theatre: How Improvisation and Street Theater Emerged as Christian Outreach to the Culture of the Time, editor.

Empowering English Language Learners, co-editor with William David Spencer.

Keeping the Dream Alive: A Reflection on the Art of Harriet Lorence Nesbitt, author and editor.

Specialist Fourth Class John Joseph DeFazio: Advocating for Disabled American Veterans, editor.

Christian Egalitarian Leadership, contributing author.

An Artistic Tribute to Harriet Tubman, co-editor.

The Commission, editor.

Finding a Better Way, editor

The Christian World Liberation Front, author and editor.

Wilma Faye Mathis

An Artistic Tribute to Harriet Tubman, co-editor.

The Commission, contributing author.

Finding a Better Way, contributing author.

When Women Speak, contributing author.

Black Girl Cry, contributing author.

God's Masterpiece, author.

Martha Reyes

Keeping the Dream Alive: A Reflection on the Art of Harriet Lorence Nesbitt, contributing author.

Specialist Fourth Class John Joseph DeFazio: Advocating For Disabled American Veterans, contributing author.

Redeeming the Screens, contributing author.

Jesús y la Mujer Herida (Jesus and the Wounded Woman), author.

Jesucristo, Tu Psicólogo Personal (Jesus Is Your Own Personal Psychologist), author)

Por Que No Soy Feliz (Why Am I Not Happy?), author.

Quiero Hijos Sanos (I Want Wholesome Children), author.

The Commission, contributing author.

Finding A Better Way, contributing author.

Olga Soler

Just Don't Marry One: Interracial Dating, Marriage, and Parenting, contributing author.

Tough Inspirations from the Weeping Prophet Apocalypse of Youth, author.

Creative Ways to Build Christian Community, contributing author.

Epistle to the Magdalenes, author and illustrator.

Redeeming the Screens: Living Stories of Media "Ministers" Bringing the Message of Jesus Christ to the Entertainment Industry, contributing author.

Berkeley Street Theatre: How Improvisation and Street Theater Emerged as Christian Outreach to the Culture of the Time, contributing author.

The First Book: Nature; The Second Book: Time Travel, Adventure, Romance, Faith; The Third Book: Revelation. Revelations Series, author.

Empowering English Language Learners: Successful Strategies of Christian Educators, contributing author.

Keeping the Dream Alive: A Reflection on the Art of Harriet Lorence Nesbitt, contributing author.

An Artistic Tribute to Harriet Tubman, contributing artist.

The Commission: The God Who Calls Us to Be a Voice during a Pandemic, Wildfires, and Racial Violence, contributing author.

Finding a Better Way, contributing author.

Contents

Part 2: Successful Strategies of Christian Ministers to the Marginalized.

Acknowledgements

I WOULD LIKE TO FIRST thank my Lord and Savior Jesus Christ for sustaining and fortifying me throughout the research and writing of this book. My sincere thanks to Dr. Scott Manor and Dr. Seth Tarrer, who started me on my dissertation journey, which serves as the conduit for this book. Thank you for your patience and understanding and for helping me to cross the finish line. Thanks to Caleb Loring III for his support of this project. Peter Lynch has been very kind to help. Sharon Percy Rockefeller deserves mention for her philanthropic work.

There were many long nights and uncertain days. Without the assistance of Community Chaplin Sara Mitchell, who is responsible for me engaging with women in homeless shelters, I would not have been a part of this ministry and for that, I am truly grateful. She mentored me and other women in ways to assist the homeless community which has blossomed over the years. I am indebted to Sara for all she has done and how she continues to be an inspiration in my life. Jeanne DeFazio, a multi-talented woman (an actress of Spanish-Italian descent, English language learner instructor, and author) and also one I have the privilege of co-teaching with at Gordon-Conwell Theological Seminary. Jeanne is the epitome of love, support, kindness, and has been all of that to me down through the years. There are special individuals from my alma mater Gordon-Conwell Theological Seminary who have been a fountain of encouragement who I must thank. Dr. William David Spencer is the epitome of God's love and kindness on the earth! He and his wife, Dr. Aida Besancon Spencer, have been a resource of knowledge, strength, understanding, and prayer. Rev. Dr. James R.

Critchlow sent me that extra boost while reminding me to allow my studies to increase my availability to the LORD and His kingdom.

To all my interviewees and contributors, thanks for all your input. To my many relatives, friends, mentors, mentees, and supporters who walk along this journey with me, thank you!

Last, but certainly not least, my immediate family. To my shero and hero, Mom and Dad. You have always believed in me, and that has kept me going. Thank you for every time you stopped to check in on me, made sure I ate when I had to shut down to study, and especially when you said, "We are so proud of you." I love you both! To all my sisters and brothers, nieces and nephews, aunties and uncles, cousins, and godchildren, thanks for just being there and encouraging me from the sidelines. Finally, to my one and only son, Darnell Rodney. There have been many years of effort that led to the production of this book, and I just want to thank you for supporting me and for stopping by my office to see if I'm alright. You are a man of few words, but your actions speak and they say, Mom, I care. Love you!

—Wilma Faye Mathis

Foreword

Julia C. Davis

I PARTICIPATE GLADLY IN HOUSE of Prisca and Aquila projects because HPA's mission statement resonates with my core Christian beliefs. I stand on the "Bible as God's revelation that affects both thoughts and words, so it is plenary, historically accurate, and consistent in itself, fully reliable, and authoritative as God's revelation" (House of Prisca and Aquila Mission Statement). As I wrote in my contribution to *The Commission*:

> In over thirty years teaching racially diverse inner-city students, I applied scriptural and constitutional principles developing strategies that empowered students to mobilize and succeed in predominantly white institutions of higher education. So many of these students have acquired professional status and make a difference in their own lives and within their communities.[1]

What I love most about this book is that it identifies strategies to help the marginalized based on scriptural principles. For example, in "Empowering the Practical Lives of Homeless Women through Transformational Journaling," Dr. Mathis states:

> We are instructed to care for widows and orphans (including the homeless).[2]

(Jas 1:27 declares: "Religion that God our Father accepts as pure and faultless is this: to look after orphans and widows in their distress and to keep oneself from being polluted by the world" [NIV].)

She also writes:

---

1. DeFazio, *Commission*, xii.
2. Mathis, *Jesus Among the Homeless*, 79.

Since journaling plays a positive role in aiding recovery from drug addiction, biblical transformational journaling can also play positive roles in helping homeless women.[3]]

(Josh 1:8 explains: "This Book of the Law shall not depart from your mouth, but you shall meditate on it day and night, so that you may be careful to do according to all that is written in it. For then you will make your way prosperous, and then you will have good success" [NIV].)

Jeanne DeFazio models "Building Christian Community for the Homeless," describing a monthly meeting at a McDonald's restaurant she organized in New York City from 1989–1995. Jeanne's chapter identifies two key strategies based on scriptural principles: feeding the homeless (Heb 13:2 NIV): "Do not forget to show hospitality to strangers, for by doing so some people have shown hospitality to angels without knowing it," and providing pastoral support and spiritual encouragement for them (Rom 15:4 NIV): "For everything that was written in the past was written to teach us, so that through the endurance taught in the Scriptures and the encouragement they provide we might have hope." Martha Reyes, in "The Hosanna Foundation," explains how her counseling guidelines for the depressed and anxious are rooted in the promises of Jesus' words: (John 14:27: "Peace I leave with you; my peace I give you. I do not give to you as the world gives. Do not let your hearts be troubled and do not be afraid" (NIV). In her afterword, "Those without a Home," Olga Soler identifies scriptures mandating believers to mentor the homeless (Prov 11:14: "Where there is no guidance, a people falls, but in an abundance of counselors there is safety" (ESV).

I relate to these experienced ministers to the marginalized. I volunteer in downtown Boston praying with the homeless, distributing food and Bibles to them. As a chaplain, I have clearance to minister in hospitals and prisons. Jesus is at work through me as I pray at the bedside of a battered homeless woman and with inmates. I recommend that everyone read this book and take the scriptural principles in it to heart. Strategies based on God's word heal and transform lives.

We all need healing. Each one of us has been dealing with pandemic grief. In the midst of a pandemic and the racial violence due to George Floyd's death, my husband Dan and I flew to California to bring his older sister, Sally, back to Massachusetts because she needed our help. As an African American couple, we encountered challenges traveling to California from Massachusetts. God protected us. Sally spent the last year of her

---

3. Mathis, *Jesus Among the Homeless*, 67.

life in and out of hospital and nursing care. My beloved brother Quincey passed away recently. Dan and I traveled again to California to attend his homegoing.

Everyone is going through a grieving process during the pandemic, but homeless people are suffering profoundly.

God's word mandates believers to help the poor (Jas 1:27) and promises we are blessed when we do. Psalms 41:1: "Blessed is the one who considers the poor! In the day of trouble the Lord delivers him" (NIV). We need to help our homeless brothers and sisters especially in these challenging times!

PART 1

Identifying the Problem of Homelessness and Applying Scriptural Principles as a Solution

Summary of the Situation of Homelessness in the United States

Wilma Faye Mathis

H OMELESSNESS IS A MAJOR social problem in the United States and is adversely affecting urban communities. There is more than one official definition of homelessness. It can be defined as an "individual or family who lacks a fixed, regular, and adequate nighttime residence, meaning: (i) Has a primary nighttime residence that is a public or private place not meant for human habitation; (ii) Is living in a publicly or privately operated shelter designated to provide temporary living arrangements (including congregate shelters, transitional housing, and hotels and motels paid for by charitable organizations or by federal, state and local government programs)."[1] In January of each year, a Point-in-Time census and survey is conducted; the annual count allows communities across the United States to conduct a comprehensive census of all persons experiencing homelessness at a given point in time.[2] Based on the findings of the survey, it is estimated that as many as 3.5 million people in America are homeless each year.[3] On a single night in 2018, there were over five hundred thousand people who experienced homelessness in the United States.[4] Of these homeless people, 65 percent (358,363) were sheltered and 35 percent (194,467) were unsheltered.[5]

Metropolitan cities have larger numbers of homeless individuals than smaller cities, although homelessness is a problem regardless of size.

1. "Frequently Asked Questions," para. 1.
2. Owen, "HUD Report Finds," para. 5.
3. "How Many People Experience Homelessness," para. 9.
4. "2018 AHAR," 1.
5. "2018 AHAR," 10.

Half of all people experiencing homelessness were in one of five states: California (24 percent or 129,972 people), New York (17 percent or 91,897 people), Florida (6 percent or 31,030 people), Texas (5 percent or 25,310 people), and Washington state (4 percent or 22,304 people). Within four states, more than half of all people experiencing homelessness were found in unsheltered locations: California (69 percent), Oregon (62 percent), Nevada (56 percent), and Hawaii (53 percent). Four other states—Maine, Rhode Island, New York, and Massachusetts—sheltered at least 95 percent of people experiencing homelessness.[6] Homelessness increased in nineteen states between 2017 and 2018: "The largest increases were in Massachusetts (2,503 additional people), New York (2,394 additional people), Texas (1,762 additional people), and Washington (1,192 additional people). The largest percentage increases were in South Dakota (23 percent) and Connecticut (17 percent)."[7]

While there are no reliable statistics on the number of homeless shelters or temporary housing in the United States, it is estimated that each night, 358,363 people are sleeping in sheltered locations.[8] HUD Exchange reported there were 896,893 beds across each type of housing: emergency shelters (ES), transitional housing (TH), safe havens (SH), rapid rehousing (RRH), permanent support housing (PSH), and other permanent housing (OPH), serving people experiencing homelessness and formerly homeless people.[9] Based on the reported total of 896,893 beds, there are 389,622 beds dedicated to sheltering those experiencing homelessness 73 percent (ES), 26 percent (TH), 0.6 percent (SH), and those who need some type of emergency shelter. Those formerly homeless individuals have the remaining 507,271 beds for housing (RRH, PSH, OPH).[10] Over half of the beds are dedicated to them. Although these statistics are not perfect, they appear to be the most reliable sampling enumerating persons experiencing homelessness in shelters on a given night.

Open Minds[11] has been curious as to how many shelter beds are needed for the homeless population. This issue arises in relation to

6. "2018 AHAR," 16.

7. "2018 AHAR," 16.

8. "2018 AHAR," 10.

9. "2018 AHAR," 74.

10. "2018 AHAR," 74.

11. Open Minds is a firm providing thirty years of information, executive education, and business solutions specializing in the health and human service industry sectors

concerns regarding homeless people being arrested for sleeping in public when there are insufficient shelter beds. Incarceration violates the Eighth Amendment against cruel and unusual punishment. The question is: "How many beds are available for the homeless population nationally?"[12] With the number of beds (896,893) estimated by the U.S. Department of Housing and Urban Development (HUD),[13] will the number of beds be sufficient? "Answering that question is complicated."[14]

According to the HUD Exchange 389,622 ES, TH, and SH beds dedicated to persons experiencing homelessness (not formerly homeless) seem insufficient to provide shelter beds for people needing immediate housing. Also, the numbers do not count families who are doubled up, living in unsafe conditions, or sleeping in their cars,[15] which would increase the number with even more people. So, based on the national average, for the reported 552,830 people experiencing homelessness on a single night, both sheltered and unsheltered, the 389,622 dedicated ES, TH, and SH beds for those currently experiencing homelessness who need immediate shelter are inadequate. The national numbers may make it appear that we have enough shelter beds, but geographic variations mean that the number of beds does not always align with the need. Many cities around the country report an inability to fill existing shelter beds.[16]

An emergency shelter is a facility that primarily provides temporary shelter for homeless people or nightly shelter beds to people experiencing homelessness. These facilities will provide individuals with the basic necessities, such as a place to sleep, shower, do laundry, get clothing, and eat or assist with money for food. Some have drop-in centers with case managers who can assist with services to move beyond shelter living. Beds are given out daily on a first come, first served basis.[17] Individuals can be directed to another shelter or turned away if none are available. Transitional housing (TS) accommodates those needing temporary shelter but will provide homeless people with up to twenty-four months of shelter and supportive

---

serving complex consumers.

12. "How Many Shelter Beds Are Enough," para. 1.

13. "2018 AHAR," 74.

14. "How Many Shelter Beds Are Enough," para. 2.

15. "Basic Facts on Homelessness," para. 3.

16. "How Many Shelter Beds Are Enough," para. 3.

17. "Emergency Shelter," para. 1.

services. This will allow individuals the time to job search and apply for permanent housing while knowing they have a place to stay.

Safe havens (SH) provide temporary shelter for hard-to-serve individuals but provide more than shelter. SH are a refuge for the homeless who suffer from some type of mental illness and serve to "close the gap in housing and services available for those homeless individuals. . . who have refused help or have been denied or removed from other homeless programs."[18]

Permanent housing for the formerly homeless[19] is rapid rehousing (RRH), providing short-term rental assistance and stabilizing services. Permanent supportive housing (PSH) is long-term housing with supportive services for formerly homeless people with disabilities and often those with chronic patterns of homelessness. Other permanent housing (OPH) provides housing with or without services that are specifically provided for formerly homeless people, but OPH does not require people to have a disability.

It is disheartening to know of the significant number of homeless families that exist. In 2017, there were 57,971 homeless families with children; this accounted for 184,661 people who were homeless, representing one-third (33 percent) of the total homeless population in that year.[20] Homeless families in Massachusetts are at an all-time high. "There are close to four thousand homeless children and parents in Boston on any given night.[21] Women made up three-quarters of the adults counted as experiencing family homelessness in the 2017 PIT data, resulting in 77.6 percent being counted as experiencing homelessness in families with children.[22] Women and children are among the fastest-growing population who are experiencing homelessness, with 15 percent of children living in poverty.[23] Children within homeless families made up more than half the nation's homelessness in four states: New York, California (12 percent or 20,964 people), Massachusetts (7 percent or 13,257 people), and Florida (5 percent or 9,587 people). New York and Massachusetts were leading with very high rates of family homelessness: "In 2018, fifty-seven out of every ten thousand people

18. "Safe Havens," 3.
19. "2018 AHAR," 79.
20. "2017 AHAR," 32.
21. "Emergency Shelter," FamilyAid, 1.
22. "Homelessness in America: Focus on Families with Children," 2.
23. "Unique Challenges of Women Experiencing Homelessness," 1.

in New York and forty-four out of every ten thousand people in Massachu-setts experienced homelessness."[24]

While this project focuses specifically on women, we should note it appears more men are homeless. There are 216,211 women counted in our Point-in-Time survey as sheltered (160,024) and (56,187) unshel-tered, while there are 332,925 men in this same category. This homeless population of 549,136 does not account for the 3,694 who are transgender or non-conforming (male or female).[25] The homeless population is not equivalent to the number of emergency shelter beds. Furthermore, this signifies an insufficient number of beds available for homeless women who need emergency shelter. So where are the remaining women? We have been made aware that unsheltered women could be living in their cars, with relatives or friends, or in the streets, which is also a problem. In some circumstances this will be fine; however, there are the "hidden homeless" (people staying temporarily with friends or family) and oth-ers who are described as under-housed or "at risk" of homelessness.[26] Although homelessness includes both men and women, as mentioned, this work will focus on women who are struggling to live in homeless shelters in the Boston urban area and the issues they face extending be-yond homelessness—isolation, depression, fear, and pain.

Women who are experiencing homelessness have physical needs (food, clothes, housing) that government agencies are trying hard to meet. However, even though these existing government, social programs, and state agency systems are in place, one in ten Massachusetts residents still live in poverty. Also, there is a spiritual element that needs to be addressed to help meet the emotional needs of women who are homeless. This book will attempt to evaluate the impact of the gospel in regards to the restora-tion of hope and help to homeless women and eventually, helping these women to thrive and develop whole life patterns.

While spending time as a participant observer in Boston's Woods-Mullen Shelter,[27] getting to know the women, their routine, and some of the challenges they face in the shelter, it has become increasingly evident that there is a necessity for meeting the needs of the whole person. We may not be able to assist everyone; however, we should "never worry

24. "2018 AHAR," 38.

25. "2018 AHAR," 11. See EXHIBIT 1.3.

26. "Homelessness Questions & Answers," 1.

27. "Woods-Mullen Shelter and Services."

about numbers. Help one person at a time. And always start with the person nearest you."[28]

Through study, observation, and personal contact, both in and outside the shelter, it can be seen that the needs of homeless women are not adequately being addressed because: a) they are disconnected from family and children in meaningful ways; b) they are stripped from the community; and/or c) they are living in isolation. I understand that homeless men may share some of these same experiences; however, women have more specific challenges. Women with children often carry the burden of childcare for their children not yet in school, not to mention working while juggling how to pay for childcare and other expenses. Female health issues include pregnancy, having sufficient menstruation products, undergoing menopause, and having enough money to purchase needed over-the-counter pain relief.

Homeless women desire to integrate back into society, experience wholesome living, and find hope. This hope can come from the gospel. The gospel is the good news of what Christ has done for all humanity—the restoration of people's relationship with God. Jesus gives voice to the voiceless, face to the faceless, and identity to the marginalized and oppressed of this world.[29] Scripture is clear that the poor will always be with us (Mark 14:7), but this should not hinder our efforts to help the homeless. The church's involvement to assist women could prove helpful where our government, healthcare, housing, labor, and education systems are lacking. We are to "reach out to the homeless and loveless in their plight."[30]

Why are people homeless? According to Pine Street Inn, "there is no simple answer to this question. People who become homeless often lack access to jobs that pay a living wage; affordable housing, and/or to health care and mental health services.[31] It is presumed there are four things—housing, services, social connectedness, and prevention—that, if figured out, could end homelessness.[32] While this may be true, the lack of essentials needed for women is leaving them at an unhealthy disadvantage. I will show how

---

28. Western, "29 Inspirational Mother Teresa Quotes," #19.

29. Person, "What's the Good News," 1.

30. The Message Bible emphasizes 'homeless': "Real religion, the kind that passes muster before God the Father, is this: Reach out to the homeless and loveless in their plight, and guard against corruption from god's word (Jas 1:27 MSG).

31. "Why Do People Become Homeless," 1.

32. Olivet, "4 Simple Ways to End Homelessness," paras. 5, 8, 10, 15, 19.

homeless women are isolated, unable to sustain family relations, and existing but not thriving. A close examination of both the Old Testament and New Testament speaks to women experiencing homelessness and can help guide them to have the ability to exercise their God-given purpose in every aspect of their lives: spiritually, mentally, and physically.

In order for the church to address the homeless population effectively, it may need to revisit its hermeneutical (interpretation) and exegetical (explanation) paradigm for engaging homelessness, specifically to women. The homeless population of women in the Boston urban area will be viewed in light of a theological exegesis on how scripture can inform churches of this homeless epidemic in our communities and how we can better serve this population. The call to care for those in need resounds throughout scripture. What do biblical teachings have to say regarding the homeless, poor, and oppressed? Chapter 2 discusses the challenges among homeless women and explores the biblical foundation for caring for the needy. In chapter 3, we look at Ruth, a woman who forsakes her pagan heritage to cling to the people of Israel. She gave it up to follow her mother-in-law Naomi, her God, Yahweh, and the Jewish customs. Ruth had no social status and economic means to survive, making her situation analogous to the homeless women of today. Chapter 4 explores Hagar in the book of Genesis and how she is representative of an outcast, as many homeless women in today's society are also regarded. Hagar's encounter with God in the desert brought her to a place of knowing God as the one who sees and hears her affliction. The responsibility of the church to homeless women should also be attentive to seeing and hearing the cries of homeless women. Chapter 5 looks at the ministry of Jesus in the Gospel of Luke, addressing the homeless and those who were rejected from society. The sick and disabled were oftentimes alienated, outcast, and marginalized. This is how the hemorrhaging woman is viewed in this text. However, Jesus heals the woman of her blood issue and gives her a sense of dignity. The chapter concludes that Christ's ministry today is to do as he did and preach the gospel to poor and homeless women. "Bring good news to the poor" (Isa 61:1) and "set at liberty those who are oppressed" (Luke 4:18). Chapter 6 will follow with what was learned. Then, chapter 7 explains how Christian community is an effective strategy to help the homeless. Chapter 8 describes ways to help street children adapt to a healthy life. Chapter 9 explains transformational journaling as a proven way to empower homeless women.

2

Challenges and the Homeless Women Among Us

Wilma Faye Mathis

It was actually a shock to me to see in the middle of the afternoon, in the middle of one of the busiest streets in this city, this human form," says Schmalz. "It jolted me." The pause immediately brought a passage from Schmalz's faith to mind—Matt 25. A portion of the Bible where Jesus instructs his followers to treat "the least of these" as they would him. "It was almost a eureka moment, where I interpreted that sight as something deeply spiritual," says Schmalz. "I was left believing that I just saw Jesus. And it was something that would not leave me."

"The fascinating thing about the Gospel is it unfolds like theater," says Schmalz. "Likewise my sculpture does the same interesting twist. When one approaches the Homeless Jesus . . . it's only till you get closer to the sculpture that the center of the feet have the ruins of being on a cross that you have that eureka moment. . . That's where the sculpture becomes like theater.[1]

---

1. Taylor, "'Homeless Jesus,'" 1–11.

Homeless Jesus, by artist Timothy Schmalz of suburban Toronto

S CHMALZ COMPARES HIS SCULPTURE to the comments made in Matt 25 where Jesus is asked about when he was homeless or needed help. When we observe closely, the case could be made that "the least of these" are not only Christians but all who are marginalized, and more specifically, homeless women. While focusing on the homeless shelter, I realized that the church and Christians are to consider being the gospel in action: "The Church can be transformed by becoming the generous and welcoming community that God commands."[2] Jesus desires for us to put our faith into action! "Whatever you did for one of the least of these brothers and sisters of mine, you did for me" (Matt 25:40 NIV). For me, this reflects the gospel in action. This is how we increase our love for the homeless, care for them, and meet them where they are. I live in the city of Boston and encounter homelessness daily. While driving to work, I have seen people who are facing and experiencing homelessness stationed at traffic lights with cups; some will wash windows and hope drivers are courteous to give a tip. Going for a walk at lunchtime, I pass the homeless on the sidewalks, in building corners, at park benches, and near public restrooms. Following the command of Jesus to give to all who ask (Matt 5:42, Luke 6:30 NIV), two of my professors, William and Aida Spencer, give out V-8 juice. Another

2. Starlight Ministries, para. 4.

professor, Jim Critchlow, gives snacks, cookies, and raisins. While I desire to give more, it is not always possible since I travel this route every day. I will help as often as possible and donate to shelters regularly, but sometimes it feels that this is not enough.

However, something happened in 2014 while I was recovering from surgery. Being limited in activities but needing to do something, I reached out to a Christian community center, Emmanuel Gospel Center,[3] where I studied while working on my master's degree. I became a certified volunteer and began assisting in Bible study at a 450-bed co-ed shelter[4] and later volunteered at a women's shelter, conducting journaling workshops to encourage the women there. Journaling is often used in recovery and as an aid to change. During these sessions, we provide a safe haven for women to talk about topics important to their lives, and we invite them to prayer, making scripture applicable to their lives, with the hope that change will occur in the company of Christians.

Outlining the Problem

It is clear that while emergency shelters (ES) are critical for those experiencing homelessness, they are not a permanent solution. Many women have been driven to shelters voluntarily, some involuntarily, and all for numerous reasons. As a result, women have been left bitter, heartbroken, desperate, and disappointed, mainly with themselves. Through observing and listening to the varied stories of homeless women, I find they experience their lives on a day-to-day basis filled with many dynamics—a haunting past, a dim future, stifling isolation, and rampant hopelessness. Everyone needs hope, especially those who are living homeless, experiencing uncertainty, not knowing each day whether they will have a bed to sleep in, let alone a home. Desperation fills the air and fear roams the halls. Their dreams are shattered and yes, many have just given up.[5] This became evident at the Woods-Mullen Homeless Shelter where I volunteer. While we journal with the women, it is clear that a long-term goal is out of reach for many. You may ask, "Why might this be?" They will write about their goals but often find it difficult to believe they will ever reach them. The focus is usually on the immediate (housing, peace, and safety), which we often hear in their spoken

3. Emmanuel Gospel Center.

4. Difazio, "Long Island a 'Big Piece' of How Boston Plans to Fight Opioid Crisis."

5. Eichstedt, "Give Me Shelter," 48–51.

prayer requests. Dreams for a better future are what each woman wants. However, under the present circumstance, most want a place to call home, to experience peace of mind, and to feel safe from the hostile environment of the shelters. Later, we will view a biblical figure, Hagar the Outcast, who desired peace of mind, despite having little.

"Poverty and homelessness are strongly correlated and loss of income acts as a major factor associated with homelessness."[6] Some earlier scholarship helps us to see the poverty crisis which often leads to homelessness is more visible today than it was over fifty years ago. Peter Drier recognizes the contributions to the war on poverty by the late Michael Harrington over fifty years ago (March 1962) from his book *The Other America: Poverty in the United States*.[7] Harrington conducted "a haunting tour of deprivation in an affluent society—that inspired Presidents Kennedy and Johnson to wage a war on poverty." "The fate of the poor," he realized, "hangs upon the decision of the better-off." The analysis gathered from Harrison is that "he wanted his book to tug at people's consciences, to outrage them and to push them to action. . . that poverty was caused and perpetuated by institutions and public policies, not by individuals' personal pathologies."[8]

Since poverty and homelessness are closely related, author, journalist, and political and social activist Barbara Ehrenreich, in her book *Nickel and Dimed: On (Not) Getting by in America*, decided to join the millions of Americans working at poverty-level wages to assess the popular view that any job leads to a better life. In her journey in the working class through Florida, Maine, and Minnesota, she recognized that poverty is harmful and damaging. "There are no secret economies that nourish the poor," she notes; "on the contrary, there are a host of special costs."[9] She observes poverty as a vicious cycle and for some, their journeys "went on to include bouts of homelessness".[10] Some women struggled to get by and did not experience homelessness, but called "home a car or a van." She also witnessed "illness or injury that must be worked through because there's no sick pay or health insurance and the loss of one day's pay will mean no groceries for the next."[11] She noted "such is certainly by no means a sustainable lifestyle,

6. "Poverty," para. 1.
7. Harrington, *In the Other America*.
8. Dreier, "Poverty in America," paras. 1, 3, 21.
9. Ehrenreich, *Nickel and Dimed*, 27.
10. Ehrenreich, *Nickel and Dimed*, 133.
11. Ehrenreich, *Nickel and Dimed*, 214.

but rather, "a lifestyle of chronic deprivation and relentless low-level pun-ishment, but rather by almost any standard of subsistence, emergency situations." Supporting oneself at these bare minimum levels, I agree, is how we should see poverty, "as a state of emergency."[12] In many cases, such deprivation leads to homelessness for so many low-wage Americans. The three most cited reasons for family homelessness are: 1) lack of affordable housing, 2) unemployment, and 3) poverty.

A Massachusetts study "found that 92 percent of homeless women had experienced physical and/or sexual assault. More than half of these women were also survivors of domestic violence and are also more likely to have experienced childhood abuse than men."[13] "Domestic violence puts women at risk of becoming homeless since abusers often isolate them from sup-port networks and financial resources."[14] Women are a minority in shelters, and for those having experienced domestic violence, they have oftentimes been placed into mixed shelters (male and female) and now feel unsafe. Nationally, more than 80 percent of women with children who experience homelessness have experienced domestic violence.[15]

Many suffer as victims of abuse: sexual, physical, psychological, and financial. The difficulty of living on the streets, finding shelter, and seeking ways for survival creates a great amount of stress on those facing homeless-ness. They "may additionally develop psychiatric conditions in response to the harsh lifestyle of feeling threatened by violence, starvation, and lack of shelter and love."[16] While 30 percent of homeless people overall suffer mental illness, the rate is significantly higher in female populations. It is es-timated that between 50 percent and 60 percent of homeless women suffer mental and emotional disturbances, often pre-dating their homelessness,[17] and "are more likely to have post-traumatic stress disorder, depression, anxiety, and other mental health disorders than other American women."[18] Moreover, research shows that substance abuse is both a cause and often the result of homelessness. Homeless women, in particular, suffer unique gender-based trauma, contributing to the higher drug use than among

12. Ehrenreich, *Nickel and Dimed*, 214.

13. "Lack of Services," para. 7.

14. "Lack of Services," para. 8.

15. "Homelessness in America," 8.

16. "Homelessness and Addiction," para. 2.

17. "Homelessness and Addiction," para. 1.

18. "Lack of Services," para. 8.

men.[19] Approximately "38% of homeless people were dependent on alcohol and 26% abused other drugs."[20] Sadly, as the homeless population increases, addiction is closely associated.

Anonymity and neglect are further problems. Individual women and girls tend to go unnoticed because they are more likely to be in a shelter or another housing program and not seen on the streets. They are known as I stated earlier, the "invisible population."[21] This invisibility of individual women and girls simply means they are "less visible." This causes them to go unnoticed because "the majority of the services and programs set up to help the homeless were made in response to the larger homeless men population."[22] As a result of women going unnoticed, the "properly funded government programs geared toward the causes of homelessness and the different life experiences for homeless women are not common."[23] Since there are 77% of women in families with children (girls), the "lack of gender-specific services for the homeless affects both individual women and families."[24] This dearth of restorative alternatives often leaves women challenged, and the staff at homeless shelters unable to address their specific needs.

Solutions to aid in the efforts to end homelessness in the Boston area are ongoing. Rosie's Place, founded in 1974 as the first women's shelter in the United States, is a sanctuary for poor and homeless women; they provide a safe and nurturing place, creating solutions for twelve thousand women a year through housing, education, and support services.[25] According to Rosie's Place, the solutions to ending homelessness "require the political will and the resources to address the causes of homelessness and barriers to permanent housing."[26] The Oxford English Dictionary defines "political will" as "the firm intention or commitment of a government to carry through a policy, especially one that is not immediately successful or popular."[27] This appears to impact why homelessness is not easily resolved.

19. "Homelessness and Addiction," para. 5.

20. "Substance Abuse and Homelessness," para. 2.

21. Stickel, "Hidden Side of Homelessness," para. 15.

22. "Lack of Services," para. 3.

23. "Lack of Services," para. 4.

24. "Lack of Services," para. 4.

25. "Who We Are," para. 1.

26. "Why We're Here," para. 4.

27. Funkhouser, "What People Get Wrong about 'Political Will.'"

Finally, when referring to political will, included are safety net programs and welfare reform, which were intended to help low-income families and children. Achieving the goal of ending homelessness will require the help of "safety net programs which are critical in mitigating the impact of poverty on women and families."[28] The effects of welfare reform were intended to reduce the number of individuals on government assistance. But over time it left families, especially with children, unable to find work without a safety net, resulting in a lack of housing, especially for women, with a sharp rise in rent that those facing homelessness are unable to afford.

Starlight Ministries is another organization that believes, particularly in Massachusetts, that "the Church can be transformed by becoming the generous and welcoming community that God commands."[29] Friends of Boston's Homeless believes homelessness can be solved with innovative, solutions-oriented programs which have "proven track records that help homeless individuals transition from the streets and shelters to lead stable independent lives in dignified housing."[30] The focus is on removing the final barriers of transition (stepping out of homelessness) that city and state programs often do not have the means to cover. However, this solution does require help from foundations, charitable organizations, and churches to bridge the gap between the public sector and the current needs of the homeless.

The homeless, especially women, are at a vulnerable place in their lives, and the role of spirituality can have an impact on them emotionally and mentally: "People who have good emotional [and mental] health are aware of their thoughts, feelings, and behaviors. They have learned healthy ways to cope with the stress and problems that are a normal part of life."[31]

In my experience with homeless women, one of the key areas plaguing them is the experience of being hurt and betrayed. However, when allowed to talk through their issues, and to understand the importance of forgiveness, some of the women experienced freedom taking place within. As Christians, we have a responsibility to the homeless in our communities. We will need to position ourselves to empower the homeless to maximize their potential to live their best lives. If we were to exemplify Jesus, we see that he did not always wait for the homeless to come to him, but, as the sculpture amid the

28. "Why We're Here," para. 4.
29. "Our Challenge," para. 2.
30. "About Friends," para. 1.
31. "Mind/Body Connection," para 1.

city illustrates, Jesus carried the good news to them. Many homeless people have heard the gospel, but fewer have seen it lived out.

How can we be the gospel in action? Paul states in Phil 1:27 to "conduct yourselves in a manner worthy of the gospel of Christ" (NIV). Living out the gospel is an act of love. I am certain if Jesus were visibly on earth today, he would certainly take time for the homeless because he loved them. Jesus has now left the work of the kingdom in the capable hands of the church that believes in him, that we will also do the works that *he* did; and greater works than these will *we* do (John 14:12 NIV). So, churches with space can consider providing beds for women to sleep at night. If space is a limitation, collaboration can be an option. This act of love can provide homeless women a safe environment, a nourishing meal, spiritual guidance, and needed resources as they continue to matriculate back into society. When we sit and listen to homeless women and show we genuinely care, we have already accomplished a major step towards reaching them, hence, the building of trust. The gospel is powerful. We observed this from the sculpture of the 'homeless Jesus' which is a representation of the gospel within the city. But how the church responds with its methods of bringing the gospel to the homeless will have an impact on whether the gospel is received at all. Since the foundation of the gospel is love, the church should also operate in love to be effective in reaching the homeless. We must go into the midst of the homeless, bring the gospel, let the love from our lives touch their lives, and allow hope to be made alive.

Biblical Foundation for Caring for the Needy

Some eager first-year seminarians took time to pull out every place in the Bible referencing the poor and needy (homeless). In amazement, the second most prominent theme in the Old Testament, found in several thousand verses, was about the poor and God's response to injustice, and the first theme was idolatry. While these two themes were often related, there is also a similarity in the New Testament. One out of every sixteen verses addresses two issues: the poor or the subject of money ("mammon" as the Gospels call it).[32] As Pope Francis notes, "Poverty is precisely at the heart of the Gospel. If we were to remove poverty from the Gospel, people would understand nothing about Jesus' message."[33] While the

32. Wallis, *God's Politics*, 212–14.

33. Glatz, "Pope Francis," Jun 16, 2015.

efforts of these seminary students were to find references to poor people, poverty, injustices, and oppression, the result was to respond to each of these biblical themes for the people of God. Why is it that pulpit sermons on the poor are lacking, while this theme inundates the Bible?[34] This is a question for our society today.

When we tend to think about poor people, we oftentimes associate them with the homeless. The plight of the poor is the second most prominent theme in the Bible; it also has its root in the Ancient Near East world. Caring for widows, orphans, and the poor in both legal and wisdom literature was a common policy in the Ancient Near East. In Mesopotamia, in the twenty-fifth century BC, King Urukagina held to the policy "that mighty people were not allowed to do injustice to the orphans and widows."[35] The famous Code of Hammurabi (1728–1686 BC) builds upon this policy. In his prologue, the king affirms "that the strong are not allowed to oppress the weak." Similarly, in his epilogue, he adds, "to give justice to the orphan and the widow."[36] The observation here is that "religious and social ethics are closely connected."[37] The weak are protected both vertically and horizontally: vertically from the god (religious sphere), horizontally from the king (social sphere).

In Egypt, material concerning widows, orphans, and the poor are restricted in legal literature, but protection of the weak was the ideal among kings and monarchs, as referenced in the wisdom literature: "Respect for the rights of the weak, widow, and the orphan flourished in times of decay or at the beginning of a new period."[38] We find evidence at the end of the First Intermediate Period and the beginning of the Middle Kingdom (circa 2000 BC) by a monarch named Ameny who boasted that he ruled his province with justice, respecting the poor man's daughter and the widow.[39]

While Ancient Near Eastern data help to support how it is humanly right for society to care for those who are less fortunate, Egyptologists such as K. A. Kitchen state: "Old Testament scholarship has made only superficial use of Ancient Near East data,"[40] finding there is little direct evidence of

---

34. Wallis, *God's Politics*, 212.

35. Fensham, "Widow, Orphan, and the Poor," 130.

36. Fensham, "Widow, Orphan, and the Poor," 130.

37. Fensham, "Widow, Orphan, and the Poor," 130.

38. Fensham, "Widow, Orphan, and the Poor," 130.

39. Gardiner, *Egypt of the Pharaohs*, 129.

40. Kitchen, *Ancient Orient and Old Testament*, 24.

the connection between the Egyptian and the Hebrew texts.[41] While some mid-twentieth scholars such as Kitchen may claim that "Old Testament scholarship has made only superficial use of Ancient Near East data," it is flooding into Old Testament scholarship, shaking up all kinds of long-held beliefs and conventional understandings of the ancient world of the Old Testament. Over the past twenty years, several scholarly works have appeared on the historiography of the Ancient Near East.[42]

We see similar regard for the protection of the weak (widows, orphans, the poor, the homeless) in Mesopotamian and Egyptian societies, and we see that their religious and social ethics are closely intertwined. However, widows, orphans, and the poor had little to no legal rights and could be subjected to oppression while their oppressors went without legal consequences.[43] The Ancient Near East needed a balance in society that not only provided legal protection but also consequences for anyone who did not adhere to the common policy.

When we turn to the Hebrew world in the Old Testament, we find numerous references to the protection and caring for the widow, orphans, and the poor. The important difference between the Ancient Near East policy and Old Testament is that the God of Israel is regarded as the only true judge and protector of the weak. This is evident when viewed in light of Ps 82:3–4 (NIV). as the God of Israel challenges the other gods to give justice to the weak, maintain the right of the afflicted and destitute, and to deliver them from the hands of the wicked. When the gods failed to do so, God declares, "like men you shall die" (Ps 82:5 NIV). Such verses illustrate and define the major difference between the Old Testament and the Ancient Near East policy. As F. Charles Fensham explains, "The exercising of justice is narrowed down to one God and all others are excluded."[44] God is the one who could ultimately bring justice and deliverance to the poor and weak of society: "The vertical line to God is clearly linked to the horizontal line to the poor."[45] When God gave the law to Moses, it was commanded that Israel care for the orphans and widows, and failure to do so resulted in severe consequences (Ex 22:21–24; Deut 27:19; Ps 68:5; Prov 15:25 NIV).

41. Chavalas, "Comparative Use of Ancient Near Eastern Texts," 5.
42. Hoffmeier, *Israel in Egypt*, 10.
43. Thurston, *Widows*, 14.
44. Fensham, "Widow, Orphan, and the Poor," 135.
45. Fensham, "Widow, Orphan, and the Poor," 135.

As this motif in the Israelite community was actualized through the high ethical religion of Yahweh and became an intricate part of the religion, it would later also be inherited by the first generation of Christians.[46] Likewise, in the New Testament, James the brother of Jesus relates caring for orphans and widows as part of "pure religion" (Jas 1:27 NIV). Richard Patterson, in his discussion on the widow, orphan, and poor in the Old Testament, concludes the reason for this prominent motif: "In purely human terms, it is perhaps understandable that the weak and the helpless of society who were so easily victimized would be the special objects of concern by an ideally righteous king."[47]

In both the Old and New Testaments, there are several Hebrew and Greek words concerning the "poor." The following will expand upon the meaning of select words that better represent the poor and homeless being addressed throughout this book.

Definitions

POOR

Out of the multiple words for poor in the Old Testament, the words that will be focused upon for this book are *ani* and *dal*. עָנִי *ani*: overwhelmed by want, poor, wretched, unfortunate, without property, needy.[48] This means to be depressed, afflicted in circumstances, mind, and body.[49] דַל *dal*: low, poor, helpless, powerless, insignificant, downcast, sullen.[50] This refers to when one has become exhausted, low, wasted, and weak in substance or natural strength.[51]

In the New Testament, the Greek word πτωχός, transliterated *ptōchos* for "poor," means economically disadvantaged, begging, needy, dependent on others for support, beggar, or destitute.[52]

---

46. Fensham, "Widow, Orphan, and the Poor," 139.

47. Patterson, "Widow, Orphan, and the Poor," 10.

48. Holladay, *Concise Hebrew and Aramaic Lexicon*, 278.

49. Wilson, *Wilson's Old Testament Word Studies*, 318.

50. Koehler et al., *Hebrew and Aramaic Lexicon*, 221.

51. Wilson, *Wilson's Old Testament Word Studies*, 317.

52. Bauer et al., *Greek-English Lexicon*, 896.

Widow

The Old Testament word אַלְמָנָה, transliterated *'almânâh*, refers to widows who are often bound to silence, helpless, oppressed.[53] The Hebrew word is related to an Aramaic word that means "to be in pain." Therefore, the widow was "the silent one."[54]

Common Greek usage for the word "widow," transliterated *chera*,[55] derived from the Indo-European root *ghe* meaning "forsaken," which may refer to any woman living without a husband, or a person "left empty" or "without."[56]

Homeless

We find in the Old Testament, specifically Is 58:7, מָרוּד, transliterated *marud*, which means homelessness, wanderer, restlessness, straying, refugee, and poor,[57] or the condition of a person being driven from home or having no home.[58] *Marud* is also the state or condition of going from place to place with no particular plan, as a condition of poverty and one who is destitute.[59]

Homeless in the New Testament is ἀστατέω, transliterated *astateo*: to be never at rest. It is also to be unsettled, a wanderer, without permanent residence, as described in 1 Cor 4:11 (NIV).[60]

We can see from both the Old Testament and New Testaments the similarities between the poor, the widowed, and the homeless. Each is needy, helpless, without, and in most instances, restless and wandering, much like the homeless population of today. Poverty and homelessness are intricately linked.

The Bible makes two important references to the homeless: ". . . we are poorly dressed and buffeted and homeless" (1 Cor 4:11 NIV), and "to share your bread with the hungry and bring the homeless poor into

---

53. Holladay, *Concise Hebrew and Aramaic Lexicon*, 58.

54. Thurston, *Widows*, 9.

55. Kittel, *"Widow"* in *Theological Dictionary of the New Testament*, 1313.

56. Thurston, *Widows*, 9.

57. Brown et al., *Hebrew and English Lexicon*, 924.

58. Wilson, *Wilson's Old Testament Word Studies*, 277, 68.

59. Swanson, *Dictionary of Biblical Languages with Semantic Domains*, 216.

60. Liddell et al., *Greek-English Lexicon*, 260.

your house" (Isa 58:7 NIV). The condition of the homeless also relates to the widow and the poor, for each of these groups is often left vulnerable, economically disadvantaged, and in need of support. All of them are considered the "silent ones."

Thus, members of each of these groups—widows, the poor, the homeless—are often classified together. The Old Testament scriptures are inundated with references to them. When we look at Adam and Eve, they can even be seen as homeless once they were banished from their home in the Garden of Eden. The Israelites on their journey through the wilderness were homeless for forty years. And Ruth the Moabite was also a homeless widow.

We have previously seen that widows were recognized in several laws designed for their protection and even survival;[61] however, the laws were not without fault. We will observe in our discussion of Ruth how God has a special concern for the marginalized, which includes the widows who were without, helpless, and wandering, and he makes provisions in providing for their well-being.

---

61. Perkins, "Widow," 2141.

3

Ruth, the Marginalized

Wilma Faye Mathis

Exegesis of Ruth

W HEN WE LOOK AT the Hebrew word for widow, *'almãnah,* we see a vulnerable group who had no inheritance or status and no law that provided unlimited protection. God, being concerned for the plight of widows, gave a warning to those who abused them: "My wrath will burn, and I will kill you with the sword" (Exod 2:24 NIV). This is how much God cared for those who were helpless, and unable to provide for themselves.

Following the death of her husband and sons, Ruth's mother-in-law, Naomi, decides to leave Moab and head back to her homeland because news came that there was food in Bethlehem (Ruth 1:6). Ruth decides to stay and accompany her widowed mother-in-law, Naomi. However, Ruth becomes a foreigner (the Hebrew word "*ger,*" alien, sojourner, stranger), now living within Jewish culture.

The book of Ruth, specifically where it is placed in the Bible, has significance. In the present-day Jewish Bible, Ruth appears as the second of the five scrolls (Song of Solomon, Ruth, Lamentations, Ecclesiastes, and Esther),[1] whereas in the Christian Bible, Ruth is placed between the book of Judges and 1 Samuel, probably due to the first clause of Ruth: "in the days when the judges ruled." This placement affects the reader's expectations regarding the nature of the book.[2] To the original reader, Ruth was understood on both a macro and micro level. At the macro level, the narrative forms a bridge between the "years when the judges ruled" (Ruth

---

1. Wigoder, *Illustrated Dictionary and Concordance of the Bible,* 830.
2. Powell, *HarperCollins Bible Dictionary,* 897.

1:1) and the monarchy of King David (Ruth 4:18–22).[3] The mention of David in 4:17 and the genealogy may give a clue as to the time the book was written: it appears that it was written when David was prominent in Israel—thus sometime during or after his reign.[4] At the micro level, "The story centers on urgent family issues and Ruth's reinterpretation of three Mosaic laws: gleaning, levirate, and kinsman-redeemer."[5] This is where our focus will be centered.

Ruth was away from her family, with no husband and no children, and was living in poverty. She was not only a widow, but she also had no son(s) to make provisions, nor a kinsman from her deceased husband to marry her, which left her "stereotypically vulnerable and thus in need of special legal protection."[6] Ruth was childless and a widow, the portrait of a widow with bleak prospects during this time. Women were inferior to men, not bound by the commandments. Schools were solely for boys. Thus, being a widow was the most feared fate. It was a disgrace; widows were expected to wait for levirate marriage (marriage to a brother of her husband or nearest kin (Deut 25:5–10 NIV). A widow's lot was unhappy and piteous. Although undue severity against her was prohibited, along with strangers, orphans, and the poor, she was commanded to the charity of the people.[7] When Naomi returned to Bethlehem she lamented, "Do not call me Naomi [pleasant] but call me Mara [bitter], for the Almighty has dealt very bitterly with me. I went away full, and the Lord has brought me back empty. . . . the Almighty has brought calamity upon me" (Ruth 1:20–21 NIV). Naomi and Ruth were classified as marginalized and considered "among the lowest, most disadvantaged classes in the ancient world. . . where you had no one to support you"[8] and could be named among "the least of these" (Matt 25:40 NIV).

Provisions for the Poor

Widows were dependent on others for provisions. One of the ways to obtain food was through the system of gleaning, the Hebrew word לקט

3. James and Barthomoew, *Finding God in the Margins*, 74.

4. Brandt and Kress, *God in Everyday Life*, 13.

5. James and Barthomoew, *Finding God in the Margins*, 74.

6. Hiebert, "Biblical Widow," 125–41.

7. Thurston, *Widows*, 12–14.

8. Guzik, "Study Guide for Ruth 1," Section A. #2.

laqat. This means to gather, to collect piece by piece (as in scraps of food), and to pick up and keep the remnants.[9] The custom of that day allowed the poor to follow the reapers in the field and glean the fallen spears of grain, as strikingly illustrated in the story of Ruth (Ruth 2:2–23).[10] God's law for his people was what made provision for the poor, the widow (Deut 24:19–20 NIV), and the foreigner. Social justice was built into the institution of gleaning for the poor (Lev 19:9–10; 23:22, Deut 24:19–22 NIV). The institution of this system served as a safeguard against the deprivation of the poor. This system provides the background of our twenty-first century welfare system, wherein we donate food to local food banks and clothing to various drop-off locations, allowing the poor and homeless to receive necessary provisions. Those of us who have compassion for the marginalized will sponsor food drives, and churches often have food pantries with allotted times for people facing homelessness in their neighborhoods and communities where they can obtain food.

Although gleaning was a means of obtaining food for the poor, Ruth's status as a foreigner meant that she had to exercise precautions. Having no family or someone to advocate on her behalf, Ruth might discover gleaning in the open fields could be risky and dangerous (Ruth 2:2). However, Ruth finds herself gleaning in the fields of Boaz, a descendent from her late father-in-law's family, who she later realizes is a near relative to Naomi. Within the social structure of that day, family members stood for each other as a form of social security.[11] In Israel, such a person was known as a *goel*[12] the kinsman-redeemer. The *goel* was the one charged with the duty of restoring the rights of another, avenging any wrongs (Lev 25:48, 49; Num 5:8; Ruth 4:1 NIV), and with whom the right of redemption lay (Num 35:19, 21; Ruth 4:1–3 NIV).

Kinsman-Redeemer

Boaz, Naomi's near relative, (2:1–3) responds to the call as Ruth's kinsman-redeemer. He promises to protect and provide her with food (3:14–15). However, there is someone else obligated to Ruth who has first rights. Once

9. Holladay, *Concise Hebrew and Aramaic Lexicon*, 535.

10. Bromiley and Patch, "Gleaning."

11. Stafford, *NIV, God's Justice.*

12. Brown et al., *Hebrew and English Lexicon*, 145. *Goel:* "To redeem, act as a kinsman, do the part of next of kin."

he learns of the obligation of redeeming Ruth, the unnamed relative declines (4:1–6). Although the nearer relative declines to redeem Ruth, the widow, from her distress, this opens the door for Boaz to do his part as kinsman-redeemer, including accepting Ruth as his wife. As kinsman-redeemer, Boaz's act of providing care, protection, and redemption is a display of God's justice. The story of Ruth is a reminder of how God's mercy, or loving-kindness, extended to everyone, including non-Israelites:[13] "It has been said that the health of a community is measured in how it treats those who are vulnerable."[14] God's church should be willing to act as a kinsman-redeemer for the homeless. While we are to pray, we are also here to reverse the unjust situations of those who are marginalized. When our world systems fail and are unable to fulfill their obligations, we have a responsibility to the poor women, widows, orphans, the jobless, and the homeless.

Church's Interpretation

Ruth is often viewed as a beautiful love story. The book of Ruth is taught in some of our churches, portraying Ruth as the church and Boaz, a type of Christ. While there are truths in these depictions, there is more to uncover. Some depictions of the story of Ruth have influenced how women see themselves, says Carolyn James:[15] "Even when Ruth does something remarkable and brave, evangelicals have tended to turn her story into a romance and Boaz into the hero who comes to rescue her. Nothing could be further from the truth."[16]

Theme of Ruth

Love is a theme in the Book of Ruth, but not with a focus on romantic love. It is *hesed* that occurs and is demonstrated repeatedly within the narrative of Ruth and underpins the narrative. *Hesed* has often been translated "mercy" in English, but the meaning is more like "loving-kindness", "faithfulness," "covenant love." "The basic aspect of relationships between humans and between God and humans, encompassing affection, loyalty,

---

13. *Readers Digest Illustrated Dictionary*, 305.

14. Zondervan, "*NIV, God's Justice*," 325.

15. James, *Gospel of Ruth*, 52.

16. James, *Gospel of Ruth*, 52.

and responsibility. In biblical usage, the emphasis is on the quality of the relationship."[17] *Hesed* is a core character trait of God himself, describing his relationship with Israel and humanity (Exod 34:6–7 NIV). Naomi uses the word *hesed* for Ruth and Orpah's kindness towards her: 'May the Lord show *hesed* to you, as you have shown to your dead and me' (Ruth 1:8). Naomi recognizes Boaz's kindness in his treatment of Ruth (Ruth 2:20), and how Boaz praises Ruth's kindness, stating, "This *hesed* is greater than that which you showed earlier" (Ruth 3:10). It is noteworthy that both the subject and object of this *hesed* is not restricted to the Israelites but enlarged to include the foreigner and a powerless one at that. This included Ruth, who was not an Israelite but a Moabite. We are called to show *hesed* to the Moabites of our day, the homeless women. As with the Israel ties, God's mercy, which he extended to them, also obligated Israel to care for widows and others who were at a disadvantage in society (Deut 10:14–19; 24:17–22; 27:19 NIV).

RUTH OF THE TWENTY-FIRST CENTURY

We have seen how widowed women in ancient Israel were insignificant, outcast, often ignored, and poverty-stricken. If we were to relate this to the status of women in our twenty-first century, some homeless women are similar to widowed Ruth. Women are often marginalized, mistreated, and invisible. Ruth left her hometown willingly but ended up in a land that was foreign to her. There are women today who decide to leave their places of comfort to pursue what they believe is the right thing to do. Sometimes things turn out just fine, while at other times, it is just the opposite. Take a woman who married and left home with the expectation of a happy life with her new husband. Unfortunately, disaster happens, and she is left alone and without. The young lady who becomes pregnant and, against her will, is no longer able to reside at home. Where can she go? The female who is suffering at the hands of an abuser and cannot convince those she trusts that she is being violated. What can she do? Many women have been driven from places of security (homes, families, jobs, marriages) and are now living in foreign places (shelters, streets, motels). This age-old story of Ruth does not exempt women in the Kingdom of God. Rather, it contains a profound message of a woman who lost everything, and yet becomes a symbol of restoration to all women because of "God

17. Freedman et al., *Eerdmans Dictionary of the Bible*, 664.

27

who has created women not to live in the shadowy margins of men or their past, but to emerge as courageous activists for his kingdom."[18] God regarded the widow as he does homeless women, desiring for them to live in their God-given purpose, "to embrace wholeheartedly God's calling, regardless of circumstances or season of life."[19] The Lord had compassion for widows and provided ways for provision (e.g., Deut 10:18, 24:17, 27:19; 2 Sam 14:4–11; Job 24:3; Ps 94:4–7; 146:9; Isa 10:2 NIV). Today, the church, we who are his ambassadors are called to look out for the needy and poor, and that includes homeless women.

18. James, *Gospel of Ruth.*
19. James, *Gospel of Ruth.*

4

Hagar, the Outcast

Wilma Faye Mathis

Exegesis

A TTEMPTS TO DISCERN THE role of the Old Testament character Hagar, the maidservant of Sarai, have subjected the biblical text to a wide variety of disparate analytical tools.[1] While there are various types of biblical criticism (textual, literary, form, etc.), it is historical criticism that I will use to seek interpretation of the biblical text within its original context. More specifically, I will focus this section upon understanding the role of Hagar in the Abrahamic narrative in Gen 16 and 21. When we open this narrative, Gen 16 is placed between two covenants (chapters 15 and 17) that God made to Abram. Chapter 15 accounts in detail the covenant made between God and Abram, beginning with Abram's concern over lack of an offspring (15:3–6), and then God's promise of his very own son. The chapter ends with the sealing of the covenant. The covenant in chapter 17 is more explicit when God tells Abram he will be made "father of a multitude of nations." His name is changed from Abram to Abraham. He will be exceedingly fruitful, and there is a promise of the land of Canaan to both him and his offspring. Abram and every male shall be circumcised. This included every male throughout his generations whether or not he was born in Abraham's house, those who were bought from any foreigner, as well as those who are not of his offspring. Finally, Sarai is changed to Sarah.[2]

1. Drey, "Role of Hagar in Genesis 16," 179.

2. Stiles, "God Will Give You a New Name," paras. 7–8:
More significant than a name given at birth occurs when God changes a name. Abraham, Sarah, (Jacob) Israel, and Peter are a few of the new names the Lord gave to people. When God changes a name, it indicates that something new has happened or will happen to that person—a new relationship, a new character quality, or a new phase of life.

Hagar has a historical backdrop, although when she enters the scene in Gen 16, all we hear mentioned is that she is an Egyptian servant. The Egyptian name of the biblical Hagar (הָגָר) closely resembles the root of the Arabic,[3] Hājar (هَاجَر),[4] meaning *flight*. This aligns with her original name being adapted to her life circumstances and understood to mean fugitive or immigrant, which Hagar became. While the Bible gives us no history of Hagar's genealogy, according to Herbert Lockyer, legends show her origin as the daughter of Pharaoh, possibly the one who took Sarai. Hagar became very attached to Sarai and insisted to her father that she accompany Sarai when she returned with Abram. "What!" cried the king, "thou wilt be no more than handmaid to her!" But Hagar, wanting to be with Sarai, replied, "Better to be a handmaid in the tents of Abraham than a princess in this palace."[5]

Lockyer admits that while this belief is appealing, "the likelihood is that Hagar was an Egyptian slave-girl whom Sarai secured for her household while she and Abram were in Egypt."[6] Therefore, being the owner of a slave-girl, "her mistress was legally entitled to do as she pleased with her."[7] This is what we see Abram telling Sarai: "Behold, your maid is in your power, do to her as you please" (Gen 16:6). The Bible helps us to know that Hagar was not a slave-girl, but a maidservant, according to Gen 16:1: "An Egyptian maid whose name was Hagar." The Hebrew word maid שִׁפְחָה (*shiphchâh*) is defined as a maid, or maid-servant, as belonging to a mistress,[8] which is who Hagar was to Sarai.

Abram and Sarai left Egypt (Gen 12:16–20) and they settled in the city of Hebron. At this point. God promised Abram that his servant

---

We see this somewhat today when a wife takes her husband's name. It represents a change in her life, both in the eyes of God and of society.

3. Lockyer, *All the Women of the Bible*, 61.

4. "Hagar," 1.

5. Lockyer, *All the Women of the Bible*, 61.

6. Lockyer, *All the Women of the Bible*, 61.

7. Lockyer, *All the Women of the Bible*, 62.

8. Harris et al., *Theological Wordbook of the Old Testament*, 947.
   Brown et al., *Hebrew and English Lexicon*, 1046:

   Though the word seems to have had a wider use in the sense of "female slave" generally, those who are mentioned as individuals in the Old Testament are personal maids-in-waiting to a married woman. A boy born of such a union would become the heir unless the wife herself later bore a son.

Eliezer was not to be his heir, but "your own son shall be your heir" (Gen 15:2–4), whom we will later know as Isaac. Sarai, being barren, wanted a child of her own and took matters into her own hands. She gave her handmaiden Hagar to Abram to bear her a child, a custom consistent with the moral standards of that day. In the Ancient Near East, the Hammurabi Code 146 states that "if a man takes a wife and she gives a maid servant to her husband, and that maid servant bear children and afterward would take rank with her mistress; because she has borne children, her mistress may not sell her for money, but she may reduce her to bondage and count her among the maid servants."[9]

Now, this brings us to chapter 16 where the focus is on Hagar and Sarai's lack of having a child. God promised Abram that he would have a son. But in Gen 16:2 Sarai says, "The Lord has restrained me from bearing children." By this time, they had been in Canaan for ten years and still had no child. Is this the reason Sarai embraced Hagar to carry out her plan for a child? This was not God's plan, as we already heard of his covenant in scripture, but Sarai's way of using alternative means to obtain what she desired. This is not foreign to the culture of the day. Realistically, it is not foreign to our twenty-first century popular creeds: "Do what you have to do to get what you want." Sarai then gives her servant Hagar to her husband Abram to be a wife to him. An ancient equivalent to surrogate parentage. Hagar gets pregnant and begins to look down on her mistress Sarai (Gen 16:4). It appears to be pride. Hagar is pregnant now and, at least for the duration, if not anything else, she feels her status has improved; in other words, "I'm not just a servant. I carry the child of Abram, who is a prominent man and at least I will feel loved." Hagar could have been feeling lonely, neglected, and craving love. However, Sarai gets upset and blames Abram for the abuse she is suffering from Hagar. Since Hagar is Sarai's servant, she was given the power of deciding what to do with her. In turn, Sarai began abusing Hagar until she ran away. Hagar typifies the woman running away into homelessness due to mistreatment, which can sometimes come at the hand of another woman:[10] "The harshness of the force Sarai exerts upon Hagar is indicated in the passage by the verb ('nh),

---

9. Harper, *Code of Hammurabi*, code 146.

10. Freedman, *Anchor Bible Dictionary*, 18.
Hagar is forcibly exiled into the desert by Sarah's authoritative instruction and Abraham's obedience to Sarah's social authority and God's covenant.

which is also used in Exodus to indicate the suffering experience of all the Hebrews when they were slaves in Egypt."[11]

Hagar finds herself in the wilderness on the road to Shur (16:7).[12] Hagar appears to be heading back home to a place of freedom or a place of familiarity. However, right at the place of Shur, she has an encounter with the Lord. We are not told from Scripture how Hagar knew this was an angel from the Lord speaking to her, but this does show God's compassion and that he is concerned for both the Israelites and the foreigner. Out of desperation, people will run with no place to go, just like Hagar trying to escape, but on the way are stopped by an unexpected visitor. Christians and the church are the hands and feet of Jesus. We can stop alongside a woman running from the hand of an abuser and offer help, encouragement, and hope. The angel of the Lord comes to her and asks, "Where did you come from, and where are you intending to go?" (Gen 16:8). Once Hagar answers that she "is running away from Sarai, her mistress," she is told to "go back and submit" (Gen 16:9). This appears to be a bit awkward to me and others. It is a troubling question, according to Danna Fewell, "if the voice to 'return' to Sarah is really God's." She argues that "God tells her to go back" should be interrupted to ask questions: "Did God really tell her to go back, or is it her own voice as with many of today's women's voices 'to go back' because they have no other place to go and no other way to survive?"[13] This may seem logical because many of today's homeless women end up going back to the place of abuse for they have nowhere else to turn.[14] However, I have to go with what the Bible says directly: "The angel of the Lord said to her, 'Return to your mistress and submit to her' (16:9)." One can ponder why Hagar would be told to go back if the Lord is concerned for her. But the Lord does care. When he has Hagar's attention, he speaks to her in

11. Williams, *Sisters in the Wilderness*, 19.

12. Easton, *Illustrated Bible Dictionary and Treasury of Biblical History*, 628.

SHUR—an enclosure; a wall, a part, probably, of the Arabian desert, on the northeastern border of Egypt, giving its name to a wilderness extending from Egypt toward Philistia (Gen 16:7; 20:1; 25:18; Exod 15:22). The name was probably given to it from the wall (or shur) which the Egyptians built to defend their frontier on the northeast from the desert tribes. This wall or line of fortifications extended from Pelusium to Heliopolis.

13. Fewell, *Children of Israel*, 34–35.

14. "Domestic Violence and Homelessness," para. 1.

When a woman leaves an abusive relationship, she often has nowhere to go. This is particularly true of women with few resources. Lack of affordable housing and long waiting lists for assisted housing mean that many women and their children are forced to choose between abuse at home or life on the streets.

covenant language and comforts and consoles her. In his way, the Lord does this with a promise in vv. 10–12, which may be translated like this:

> I will surely multiply your offspring so they cannot be numbered
> for multitudes.
> Behold you are pregnant and shall bear a son,
> You shall call his name Ishmael,
> Because the Lord has listened to your affliction.
> He will be a wild donkey of a man,
> His hand against everyone,
> And everyone's hand against him,
> And he shall dwell over against his kinsmen.
> (Gen 16:10–12 NASB)

In that day having a son was not only a blessing but important, as women often did not have economic means once they became old, so they relied upon their sons. After studying these verses more closely, one sees that covenants are important to God. The promise of descendants to Hagar, the foreigner, is because the child's father is Abram. God seems to be taking his covenant promise to the patriarch quite seriously. In Gen 15, God made a covenant with Abram that he would have countless descendants. The fact is that Hagar is the second wife of Abram and Ishmael is her son; God will uphold his covenant and make Ishmael a great nation: "No matter that he did not instigate Hagar's conception (Sarah did). No matter that Hagar is not even a Hebrew. A son of Abram is, nevertheless, a son to Abram, and, therefore, part of the covenant."[15] So here, "the biblical writer is illustrating that by this covenant of Gen 15, God is willing to bless *any* descendant of Abram."[16]

The promise for the type of man her son Ishmael will be may present the image of him being wild but free, which is what Hagar desired for herself. Clearly as vv. 11 and 13 indicate, the Lord cares for Hagar, has heard her affliction, and has a plan for her life in her suffering. Hagar "called the name of the Lord who spoke to her" ראה *râ'âh* which means "God who sees," and a more literal translation to this passage is: "Even here have I looked behind my beholder."[17] The well between Kadesh and Bered was called Beer Lahai Roi, "the well of the Living One who sees me"

---

15. Kuruvilla, *Genesis*, 203.

16. Drey, "Role of Hagar in Genesis 16," 193.

17. Young, *Young's Literal Translation* (Gen 16:13).

(16:14). To be alone in a desert wondering if anyone cares about you has to be heart-wrenching. But to be visited by someone, in this case the angel of the Lord who calls her by name, had to be a life-changing encounter. According to the *Denison Journal of Religion*, Hagar is filling roles that are customarily applied to the patriarchs.

> Hagar's wilderness scenes are not just God showing pity toward the less fortunate, and they do not merely represent God's encompassing love for all of His creations. That Hagar speaks directly to Yahweh, names Him, and receives the promise that she will be the mother of a large nation makes it clear that she is a significant female character in the Genesis story.[18]

The combination of Gen 16 and 21 extends the Hagar story into two episodes in which Hagar repeatedly enters the wilderness as the result of family conflict over offspring and inheritance.[19] The first fourteen verses of Gen 21 are about inheritance and the threatening status of Hagar and her son. Once God blessed Abraham and caused Sarah to birth Isaac, the promised son, Abraham prepared a great feast. At this time, Sarah noticed that Ishmael was laughing in mockery at Isaac. Sarah demanded Abraham to "cast out this slave woman with her son" (Gen 21:10 NIV). She did not want Ishmael to have an inheritance with Isaac. Although this displeased Abraham, it was God who said: "Whatever Sarah says to you, do as she tells you" (21:12). For God would "make a nation of the son of the slave woman also" because he was Abraham's offspring (21:13).

Following in obedience to God, Abraham gave water and bread to Hagar and sent her and the child away, and Hagar left and wandered in the wilderness of Beersheba: "The threat of Ishmael results in the expulsion of Hagar, who at this time does not run away but is driven into the wilderness with limited provisions on her back. A crisis of water ensues *about* Ishmael, prompting intercession by Hagar and divine rescue."[20] Hagar is poor, and her limited provisions connect to the economic issue of homelessness today where women are surviving with their carts and what they have on their backs. Once the water was gone, Hagar put her child under the bushes, and stood a way off, for she did not want to "look upon the death of the child." It was when the child began to cry, God heard his voice, then the messenger of the Lord called Hagar from heaven, saying, "What troubles

18. Peecock, "Hagar: An African American Lens," 6.
19. Dozeman, "Wilderness and Salvation History," 23.
20. Dozeman, "Wilderness and Salvation History," 28.

you, Hagar?" Then God assures Hagar that "God has heard the boy where he is; go get the boy and hold onto him; I am going to make him a great nation" (21:17–18). God opens Hagar's eyes, and she sees a well of water and is able to fill her skin and give her son to drink, reviving both Hagar and Ishmael. This is the second instance where God hears שָׁמַע *shama*, which is "to listen, hear and answer." The first is Gen 16:11: שָׁמַע; when used with *el*, God heeds to a request.[21] He did this when listening to the affliction of Hagar, and here in Gen 21:17 (NIV), he "hears and listens"[22] to the voice of the child. This is a demonstration of how the Almighty God hears the cry of Hagar, Ishmael, and, by inference, of all humanity.

As Ishmael grew up, God was with him. Ishmael lived in the wilderness, became an expert with the bow, and Hagar got him a wife from Egypt. Afterward, we hear no more of Hagar (Gen 21:19–21). "In the midst of the narrative about Isaac, there is extended attention to a promise of being a great nation (Gen 16:18) and an assertion of God's abiding presence with Ishmael (Gen 16:20) even as he was with his father Abraham (Gen 16:22). However, God cares for this outsider whom the tradition wants to abandon."[23] Homeless women are oftentimes abandoned for many reasons (drugs, addiction, laziness). "As a society, we have a stereotypical view of homeless people (e.g., alcoholics, drug addicts, dangerous, mentally ill) and there is a profound stigma around being homeless in the United States. Further, targeted violence against homeless people is a serious national issue."[24] But as with Ishmael, God cares about the vulnerable homeless population. Regardless of what stereotype has been attached to them, God wants the best for their welfare and so should the church.

---

21. Holladay, *Concise Hebrew and Aramaic Lexicon*, 376.

22. Brown et al., *Hebrew and English Lexicon*, 1033.

23. Brueggemann, *Genesis*, 183.

24. "Beyond Stigma and Stereotypes," para. 1.

The U.S. Department of Housing and Urban Development (HUD) estimates that over 50 percent of the individuals living in supportive housing programs had either a substance use disorder, a psychiatric disorder, or both. Mental illness and addiction interfere with an individual's ability to build a satisfying, stable life. Without access to affordable treatment for substance abuse or psychiatric issues, many homeless men and women continue to descend deeper into a cycle of poverty, drug and alcohol use, and mental illness.

Church's Interpretation

The battle over how the stories of marginalized women of the Old Testament such as Hagar should be read stirs great controversy. While this is not the focus of my book, my reason for addressing various interpretations of the biblical text is to help alleviate the notion that the Bible supports cruelty and abuse to women, which includes homeless women. John Thompson takes steps to shed light on how texts like Hagar and others have been interpreted according to exegetical tradition "that supports the patriarchal subjugation of women and treats them as expendable—as 'throw-away characters.'"[25] The traditional Christian reads the Bible as defending God as sovereign, unveiling his plan of salvation amidst patriarchy and human failure, while contemporary feminist theology offers its critique of the Bible. Post-Christian feminist Daphne Hampton wonders why anyone would bother re-reading these stories of women and grant any authority to the text as they appear, given "the extent to which this Christian story [sic]" —namely, the story of a God traditionally seen as male—"has harmed women."[26] Daphne, while referencing the stories of marginalized women of the Old Testament, neglects to acknowledge Hagar's story and other women is an Old Testament Israelite story, not Christian. Feminist biblical interpreter Phyllis Trible, whose 1982 Beecher lectures at Yale, published under the title *Texts of Terror: Literary-Feminist Readings of Biblical Narratives*, tells stories of women such as Hagar, Tamar, and the daughter of Jephthah as she hears them, sees them as tales of terror with women as victims[27] but states her intentions were not to reject the Bible but rather its patriarchy.[28] On the other hand, Mieke Bal faults Trible for (among other things) her attempt "to exonerate [God] from the scandal caused by male characters."[29] Thompson examines numerous exegetes from the first to the sixteenth century, setting the stage with Philo and Josephus, moving to the patristic period, the Middle Ages, and the era of the Reformation, and discovers that problematic texts such as Hagar are disturbing to most exegetes, and, due to human sensitivities, the texts have tested the limits of exegetical skills. However, "the Bible is and has always been an

---

25. Blacketer, "Book Review: Writing the Wrongs," 448.

26. Hampson, *Theology and Feminism*, 4.

27. Trible, *Texts of Terror*, 1.

28. Thompson, *Writing the Wrongs*, 4.

29. Bal, *Death and Dissymmetry*, 4.

immensely important and informative text. . . . the Bible has always been seen as worth fighting over—or against."[30] We should keep in mind that the cultural context of Abraham's time, as with Paul's day, was different from that in our time. The people may have thought differently than we do today. This should be understood and taken into consideration to gain a proper interpretation of Scripture, not allowing what is happening in the text to cause us to lose focus that it is the sacred text. We should be very wary of judging the text of the word of God by our twenty-first-century depraved standards. Has our enlightened civilization really improved upon the biblical standards? I think the mistake being made is equating God with the sins of the men in these accounts, that God stands with Hagar, Tamar, Ruth, and other oppressed women is obvious and anyone without prior prejudice. God does not simply side with oppressive males, nor is God either male or female as Deut 4:15–16 (NIV) points out.

Theme of Genesis (Chapters 1–11)

The main theme in Gen 1–11 is a depiction of God as a creator over all the universe, while there are sub-themes that depict God's relationship with humanity as a whole: disobedience, the wickedness of humanity, the problem of sin, and a world in need of salvation. Genesis chapters 12–50 are about a covenant according to Gen 17:7: "And I will establish my covenant between me and you and your offspring after you throughout their generations for an everlasting covenant, to be God to you and to your offspring after you." This is a dominant theme as it explores God's relationship with Abraham (formerly Abram) and his descendants. The preceding chapters, 1–11, describe God's plan to restore a fallen and sinful people to the right relationship with himself, and in chapters 12–50, God does so through bestowing a special blessing upon Abraham.[31] A covenant, which is a solemn binding agreement between two or more parties (Gen 15, 17), involves promises, as the one God made with Abraham that, while he was childless, he would be the father of many nations, his descendants would have land, and the world would be blessed through him. This theme of promise and blessing runs throughout the narratives as they are repeated to Abraham, then to Isaac, and then Jacob. These patriarchs had the status of being chosen, and though, they were not without sin, it was God's choice

30. Thompson, *Writing the Wrongs*, 16.

31. Magnum et al., *Genesis 12–50*.

to bless them, not on any righteousness based upon their own character: "The descendants of Abraham have been called to be God's chosen people and the conduit of blessing to the world (Gen 12:3), but their internal conflicts consistently limit their effectiveness."[32] As humans, we have internal conflicts that are clashing against our struggles and desires, as we saw with Sarah and Abraham: "Indeed the message of the Jacob cycle of stories (Gen 25–36) could be summarized as God is faithful even when we mess things up again and again."[33] God's faithfulness can be seen as the overarching theological message in Genesis.

Hagar of the Twenty-First Century

Hagar is the story of a young woman in the Bible who represents thousands of homeless, poor, and even widowed women. Many women throughout the world are currently facing the Hagar challenge and, sadly, we also have Ishmaels of our day who are left somewhere weeping in isolation waiting for someone to hear their cry.

While there is much focus on homeless women and rightfully so, the children are suffering just as much as the mother. Kathleen McKiernan, an award-winning journalist focused on education, homelessness, and breaking news in the city of Boston, published an article in the Boston Herald: "Advocates worry homeless pupils' lives 'are being ignored' in crisis."[34] Here, she highlights where nearly four thousand students in Boston Public Schools are homeless. "Roughly one in every fourteen, a crisis school officials expect to get worse as the city's housing prices continue to soar and force families onto the street."[35] This rent escalation makes it difficult for low-income families to afford housing, says a spokesman for family aid in Boston which runs a shelter for families.[36] Boston is a city that cares and does a lot for people. There are people in shelters, which is good; however, many are sitting in the shadows because of "the lack of affordable housing, and we are seeing more families become homeless."[37] "It's heartbreaking," says an East Boston high school liaison. "A lot of kids

32. Magnum et al., *Genesis 12–50.*

33. Magnum et al., *Genesis 12–50.*

34. McKiernan, "Advocates Worry," headline.

35. McKiernan, "Advocates Worry," 1.

36. McKiernan, "Advocates Worry," 6.

37. McKiernan, "Advocates Worry," 6.

I see are embarrassed they are in this position. It's not easy for them. They want to appear as normal as possible."[38]

The Boston local news featured a special report: "Nearly 4,000 Students Homeless as Boston Crisis Deepens."[39] McKeirnan describes sad but real situations that are ongoing. Take for example Jose and Nicole, whose names have been changed to protect their identity. They are among thousands of teenagers and families in Boston and throughout Massachusetts who are homeless. There is always the day-to-day worry of shelters. Regularly, they are bounced from shelters to motels, sometimes ending up in a crowded motel room eating microwave meals. During such times, they are among the "roughly 300 families stashed away in a state-funded motel and hotel rooms across Massachusetts."[40] One night the family, Jose, Nicole, mom, and dad, camped out in the emergency room at one of Boston's City Hospitals where they tried to blend in among the waiting patients and hospital staff in order to have a roof over their head for the night. This family has slept on couches and floors of friends' homes, and even under bridges as the city housing prices become more and more out of reach. The mother in this case works at a daycare, but it is not enough to cover the rising costs of rents in Greater Boston for her family. The children are suffering while the parent is both struggling and suffering. Glimpses of hope come when the family is moved into a scattered-site shelter. These shelters house multiple families in one apartment building. The teenagers are at least able to work summer jobs. For a few hours a day, they feel like normal teenagers and forget they have no home. They stated, "I love it, we are distracted. . . . our minds are not on where we are going to live."[41] Then the stark reality once again fills their minds. Parallel to Hagar's experience, this family's desert comes in the form of depression, mental anguish, low self-esteem, hunger, living in places where there is already overcrowding, living in places of loneliness, which produce fear and lack of peace. This is a portrait of people who are in pain, suffering, and living a life of an outcast. However, it would be unfair to portray Ishmael and perhaps Hagar as totally innocent. Perhaps they both were mocking Isaac so that Sarah apparently feared he would be hurt and this contributed to their expulsion.

38. McKiernan, "Advocates Worry," para. 8.
39. McKiernan, "Nearly 4,000 Students Homeless," headline.
40. McKiernan, "Nearly 4,000 Students Homeless," para. 11.
41. McKiernan, "Nearly 4,000 Students Homeless," para. 19.

It appears Hagar initially may have become attached to people she admired. I also believe that she never imagined that she would be mistreated or despised; after all, she was being obedient to what was apparently right during this time. As a result, Hagar, now a helpless victim, finds herself and her child rejected and outcast. Hagar waited hopelessly in the desert, and, when she thought her life was over, she was seen by God (Gen 16:13–14). Many homeless women are living as outcasts. Not all women and their children are responsible for their situation. Many are waiting to be seen by the church, Christians, advocates, and those who care enough to help lift them out of their desert.

5

Ministry of Jesus among the
Homeless and Marginalized

Wilma Faye Mathis

W E HAVE OBSERVED IN ancient times how the poor, widows, the homeless, and women were often forsaken and unfortunately considered as the silent ones in society. In the Old Testament under the Mosaic Law, God commanded the orphans and widows to be cared for, and failure to do so resulted in consequences (Exod 22:21–24 NIV). As we saw with Ruth, God made provisions and ensured she was protected (Ruth 3:14–15), and commanded for food to be given and the homeless brought into their houses (Isa 58:7 NIV).

Historical Background—Before Jesus

Poverty is not only the lack of food or the lack of shelter or being sick and unable to receive medical care or not having the things necessary for survival, but it is the result of a progressive state of marginalization that ends up in disenfranchisement and isolation. At the beginning of the first century under the Roman government, there was no middle class: you were either an upper-class or a lower-class citizen.[1] The social and economic policy of the Roman Empire was the "Roman system of inequality."[2] By

---

1. Finley, *Ancient Economy*, 125.

The obvious difficulty with the city-state as a community, with its stress on mutual sharing of both burdens and benefits, was the hard fact that its members were unequal. The most troublesome inequality was not between town and country, not between classes, but simply between rich and poor.

2. Garnsey and Saller, *Roman Empire*, 125.

the time of Jesus, Roman rule was oppressive for Jewish people[3] and the cultural attitude of women had drastically changed from Old Testament biblical times. Jesus came to change all that! He came to change it by treating women as equals, as persons created in the image of God. Thus, I chose Luke among the other Gospels to highlight the woman with the issue of blood because of his detailed analysis and profession as a physician. Luke also emphasizes Jesus' love and respect towards women: Mary, Martha, Elizabeth, and Anna, and also that he came to bring good news that would cause great joy for all the people (Luke 2:10 NIV).

Exegesis of Luke (4:18–19; 8:43–48 NIV)

Luke shows the compassion of Jesus and his interactions with women, as with many different ethnic, religious, economic, and social groups, including the poor, the homeless, the sick, and the oppressed. While accounts of the marginalized and various women are noteworthy, my focus for this study will be on Luke's Gospel 8:43–49 and reference to 4:18–19.

Jesus in the Gospels

Jesus preached the message of good news to the whole world: whether Pharisees, tax collectors, children, lepers, prostitutes, homeless, poor, or rich, he delivered the gospel to all without prejudice. As James Hurley notes, "The foundation-stone of Jesus' attitude toward women was his vision of them as *persons* to whom and for whom he had come. He did not perceive them primarily in terms of their sex, age, or marital status; he seems to have considered them in terms of their relation (or lack of) relationship to God."[4] According to biblical scholar Walter Wink, Jesus violated the mores of his time in every single encounter with women recorded in the first four gospels. For both the oppressed and for women, Jesus came and turned the accepted wisdom of the day upside down.[5]

The gospels are replete with instances of Jesus and his encounter with women and the marginalized of the society of the day. The disciples were astonished at Jesus for talking openly to the Samaritan woman at the well

---

3. Lamerson, *Graeco-Roman Background*, para. 9.

4. Hurley, *Man and Woman in Biblical Perspective*, 83.

5. Yancey, *Jesus I Never Knew*, 154.

(John 4:27 NIV). Jesus respected the dignity of women where the law demanded judgment: The woman with the alabaster box anoints Jesus (Luke 7:36–50 NIV) and, according to tradition, he does not condemn the woman caught in adultery (John 8:3–11 NIV). Jesus advocated for the poor, crippled, lame, and blind and instructed them to be invited to dinner (Luke 14:13 NIV). Jesus also identified with the homeless. He said, "Foxes have holes, and birds of the air have nests, but the Son of Man has nowhere to lay his head" (Matt 8:20 NIV). Jesus moved from place to place and frequently stayed at the Mount of Olives (Luke 21:37; 22:39 NIV), and with Mary and Martha and Lazarus who offered him hospitality when Jesus was traveling through the village (Luke 10:38–42 NIV). Although Jesus recognized that poverty, injustices, inequality, and homelessness plagued society (Mark 17:7 NIV), in his teaching his followers were admonished to "give to the one who begs from you, and do not refuse the one who would borrow from you" (Matt 5:42 NIV). This makes it clear that Jesus' public ministry included a deep and fearless challenge to the prejudices and injustices that occurred during his day. He directly challenges social and religious attitudes that act to keep the marginalized in their places of oppression.

Jesus the Rabbi

Luke begins his account of Jesus' public ministry deeply rooted in the Jewish religious tradition of synagogue worship (e.g., his reading from the scroll of the prophet Isaiah) and Scripture-reading (e.g., the birth of John the Baptist, and the ancestry of Jesus). In his gospel, Luke establishes the basis for Jesus' entire ministry—a ministry of liberation! His gospel begins with Jesus doing a very normal and appropriate thing for a Jewish male rabbi of his time. *Rabbi* was a title of respect, meaning "my great one," or "my superior one," used in Jesus' day for Jewish religious teachers. According to Matt 23:6–8 (NASB), "They love the place of honor at banquets and the chief seats in the synagogues, and respectful greetings in the market places, and being called Rabbi by men. . . . But do not be called Rabbi; for One is your Teacher, and you are all brothers." "'Rabbi' was evidently used as a common title of address for the Jewish scribes and Pharisees; however, in the New Testament it is most commonly used as a title of respectful address when others were speaking to Jesus."[6] He was distinguished from the normal rabbi according to Matt 7:28–29 (NASB): "And when Jesus finished

6. Elwell et al., *Baker Encyclopedia of the Bible*, 1815.

these sayings, the crowds were astonished at his teaching, for he was teaching them as one who had authority, and not as their scribes."

The most common term applied to Jesus is that of the "teacher" although not specifically stated in Luke. The Greek word ῥαββί (borrowing from Aramaic) means a Jewish teacher and scholar recognized for expertise in interpreting the Jewish Scriptures.[7] With regards to meaning, the term has the unambiguous sense of "to teach," "to instruct."[8] Jesus is repeatedly referred to as such in the gospels. Jesus came to his hometown Nazareth (v. 14) and was qualified to teach in the synagogues because he was an observant Jew as evident in his clothing (Luke 8:44 NIV), his observation of the Feasts (John 2:13; 7:2,10 NIV), and his traveling up to Jerusalem as prescribed in the Torah (John 7:14 NIV). It was customary among the Jews that Rabbis and teachers such as Jesus read the Holy Scriptures publicly, interpret them, preach, and teach.[9] Jesus takes the scroll and, quoting from Isa 61:1–2 (NIV), speaks:

> "The Spirit of the Lord is upon me,
>> because he has anointed me
>> to proclaim good news to the poor.
> He has sent me to proclaim liberty to the captives
>> and recovering of sight to the blind,
> to set at liberty those who are oppressed,
>> to proclaim the year of the Lord's favor."
>
> (Luke 4:18–19)

Luke 4:18–19

Cornelius a Lapide pointed out that it was the will and guidance of God for Jesus to choose Isa 61 to show he was the Messiah whom "Isaiah described as a prophet."[10] Jesus declared himself as different than any normal rabbi

---

7. Louw and Nida, *Greek-English Lexicon*, 415.

8. Karl Heinrich Rengstorf, "Διδάσκω."
Of some 95 occurrences in the NT, roughly two thirds are in the Gospels and the first part of Acts. On the other hand, there are only ten instances in Paul (including Ephesians). Rengstorf provides us with the emphatic use of the term among the first followers and in the early church rather than in the Gentile congregations of Asia Minor or Greece.

9. Lapide, *Great Commentary of Cornelius À Lapide*, 160.

10. Lapide and Mossman, *Great Commentary of Cornelius a Lapide*, 160.

when he opened the scrolls in Luke 4 and says, "the Spirit of the Lord is upon me." In observing the words "has anointed me" in the Hebrew מָשַׁח to anoint, smear (Messiah) and Greek Μεσσίας, literally, "the anointed one," referring to Jesus as the Χριστός (Christ), Jesus was anointed at his baptism, "when Jesus also had been baptized and was praying, the heavens were opened, and the Holy Spirit descended on him in bodily form, like a dove; and a voice came from heaven, 'You are my beloved Son; with you, I am well pleased'" (Luke 3:21–22 NIV).

Also, contrary to the normal rabbis of the day, Jesus not only taught in the synagogues but taught by the lakeside and in the open fields (Matt 13:1; Luke 6:1 NIV). Especially distinctive is the way that Jesus directed his teachings; it was not only to the educated class or a particular religious group but to all, including women, children, sinners, and the poor. Jesus' message was directed toward anyone who had an ear to hear. The words of Jesus at the inauguration of his ministry describe the breadth of the church's proclamation in the city.[11] Jesus makes a mission statement that will help define and guide his ministry. Luke portrays Jesus as the bringer of "good news" (literally the word "gospel"). The Greek term used here is εὐαγγέλιον which in several languages is an expression and should be rendered by a phrase: "'news that makes one happy' or 'information that causes one joy' or 'words that bring smiles' or 'a message that causes the heart to be sweet.'"[12] Luke shows that Jesus is bringing the good news to "the poor," the interpretation in our English Bibles. However, the phrase in the Greek, ἔχρισέν με εὐαγγελίσασθαι πτωχοῖς, "to announce good news to poor" is not specific to economically poor people, "but people who have little or nothing to expect from the circumstances which determine their life and are therefore dependent upon God."[13] The omission of the article before πτωχοῖς (ptōchos), which is seen before the other nouns in this verse but not here, "shows that the reference is not to one specific group but to

---

In the English Bible, the commonly used phrase "and when he had opened the book" (Luke 4:16) is not the original. The Vulgate states, "as He unrolled the book." Which is better than the Vatablus, "when He had unfolded." There were other translations that state, "when He had spread out." This meaning of the Greek ἀναπτύσσω anaptyssō is to 'unroll a scroll. Since the books of the Hebrews consisted of a large piece of rolled parchment, "to read this parchment it was, therefore, necessary to unroll it, and spread it out."

11. Linthicum, *Empowering the Poor*, 41.

12. Louw and Nida, *Greek-English Lexicon of the New Testament*, 412.

13. *Cambridge Greek Testament*, Luke 4:18.

people who are in this situation generally."[14] This does not eliminate Jesus' concern for "the poor" and the responsibility he gives to others to care for them (Luke 12:33; 14:13; 18:22 NIV).

Jesus came to bring liberty to the captive and freedom to the oppressed. He may not have literally broken down prison walls but rather the imprisonment of people's minds and those oppressed by the devil (Luke 13:12–14, Acts 10:38 NIV). He aims to keep people impoverished to sin, but Jesus comes to bring good news. He came to heal the brokenhearted and to give recovery of sight to the blind, as with the blind man by the Jericho road (Luke 18:35 NIV) and later Saul's physical and spiritual blindness (Acts 9:18; 26:16–18 NIV). In Isa 52, the prophet speaks of the Lord's coming salvation and how God comforts Israel in its suffering with a promise of restoration. Although Israel will be taken captive, enslaved, and impoverished, God will liberate and bless his people.

Luke 8:43–49

In the book of Luke, several women are noted that the other gospels do not mention. Thirteen of them appear here and nowhere else. These women are often examples of deep piety and run the gamut from poor (the widow who gives the mite) to wealthy (Joanna) to those with a past now transformed (the sinful woman who anoints Jesus' feet).[15] Several key stories in Jesus' ministry involve women, revealing his compassion for them, his countercultural views of them, and their ability to participate in God's work. Luke gives us one particular story that would have become irrelevant to our study if Jesus had not intervened.

The Woman in the Crowd

The "woman in the crowd"[16] is how Luke refers to the hemorrhaging woman who begs Jesus for healing. She was well-entitled for several reasons: she is an invisible woman in the crowd, living in an increasingly impoverished situation and relegated to a marginal position within society. Similar to the

---

14. Reiling and Swellengrebel, *Handbook on the Gospel of Luke*, 200.

15. "Women in the Bible," para. 13.

16. Newsom and Ringe, "Mark," 267.
Tolbert refers to her as the "woman in the crowd" in his discussion on women among the healed.

homeless women who tend to go unnoticed because they are more likely to be in a shelter or other housing programs and not seen on the streets, they are considered among the invisible population. Each of the synoptic gospels (Luke 8:43–48; Matt 9:20–22; Mark 5:25–34 NIV) records her encounter with Jesus and the "discharge of blood" that she had suffered for twelve years. In his writings, Eusebius "records a tradition that she was a Gentile, a native of Caesarea Philippi."[17] The woman in the crowd had gone to the doctors to get better, for "she had spent all her living on physicians, and could not be healed by anyone" (v. 43). As a physician, Luke must have had some idea of all the money she spent trying to find a cure. The Greek term ῥύσις αἵματος is translated as "flux of blood" and also referred to as αἱμορρᾰγία "hemorrhage" from where we get "issue of blood": heavy, uncontrollable bleeding.[18] The Mosaic Law said any flow of blood, whether associated with bearing children (Lev 12:7 NIV), menstrual impurity (Lev 15:19 NIV), or continual bleeding (Lev 15:25; Luke 8:43 NIV) rendered her unclean (Lev 15:20–21 NIV). Those who were ritually unclean were separated from God and the congregation (Lev 15:31 NIV). "A woman's menstrual flow, because of its cyclic occurrence analogous to such important cosmic rhythms as the phases of the moon, its connection with fertility, and its relationship to the life forces contained in the blood, was a potent source of uncleanness. . . . analogous to, but more serious than, menstrual impurity was a persistent discharge of blood from a woman."[19] "This disease was a chronic hemorrhage, for which she had found no relief from the physicians. In his "Horae Hebraicae," John Lightfoot gives a list of the remedies applied in such cases,"[20] which seemed sufficient but, instead, she continued to suffer and become poorer. Even the ancient rabbis had many different formulas to help a woman afflicted like this. Rabbi Jochanan says:

> Take of gum Alexandria, of alum, and of corcus hortensis, the weight of a zuzee each; let them be bruised together, and given in wine to the woman that hath an issue of blood. But if this fails, Take of Persian onions nine logs, boil them in wine, and give it to her to drink: and say, Arise from thy flux. But should this fail, Set her in a place where two ways meet, and let her hold a cup of wine in her hand; and let somebody come behind and affright

17. "Mark 5:25-26—Exposition."

18. Bauer et al., *A Greek-English Lexicon of the New Testament*, 908.

19. Toombs, "Clean and Unclean," 644.

20. Spence-Jones and Exell, *Pulpit Commentaries*, 644.

her, and say, Arise from thy flux. But should this do no good. Take a handful of cummin and a handful of crocus, and a handful of foenu-greek; let these be boiled, and given her to drink, and say, Arise from thy flux. But should this also fail, Dig seven trenches, and burn in them some cuttings of vines not yet circumcised (vines not four years old;) and let her take in her hand a cup of wine, and let her be led from this trench and set down over that, and let her be removed from that, and set down over another: and in each removal say unto her, Arise from thy flux."[21]

The woman in the crowd "tries not to advertise her presence, because the hemorrhage makes her polluted and untouchable to her fellow Jews,"[22] and, labeled her as a religious and social outcast who only dared approach Jesus from behind.[23] However, in this case, the 'liberator' of the outcast and the oppressed was the cure that was needed for this woman. Contrary to expectations, the woman did not give her uncleanness to Jesus. Rather, Jesus' healing power made the woman clean.[24] Jesus can heal both body and soul, and he heals the woman of her infirmity, giving her a sense of dignity. Jesus' healing stopped not only the flow of blood, but the flow of money, resources, and wealth to physicians. Jesus was able to heal, recoup, and restore social status. So, how do I know?

The woman with a hemorrhage who was cured by our savior, as we learn from the holy Gospels (Mark 5:24–34). Her house was pointed out in the city, and amazing memorials of the Savior's benefit to her were still there. On a high stone (base) at the gates of her home stood a bronze statue of a woman on bent knee, stretching out her hands like a suppliant. Opposite to this was another of the same material, a standing figure of a man clothed in a handsome cloak and reaching his hand out to the woman. Near his feet on the monument grew an exotic herb that climbed up to the hem of the bronze double cloak and served as an antidote for diseases of every kind. This statue, they said, resembled the features of Jesus and was still extant in my time: I saw it with my own eyes when I stayed in the city. It is not surprising that those Gentiles, who long ago were benefited by our savior, should have made these things since I have examined likenesses of his apostles also—Peter and Paul—and in fact of Christ, himself preserved

21. Clarke, *Commentary on the Whole Bible*, 429.
22. Alexander et al., *Eerdmans Handbook to the Bible*, 505.
23. Butler, *Holman Bible Dictionary*, 635.
24. Butler, *Holman Bible Dictionary*, 635.

in color portrait paintings. And this is to be expected since ancient Gentiles customarily honored them as saviors in this unreserved fashion.[25]

The Hem of His Garment

According to the Mosaic law, every Jew was obliged to wear a fringe or tassel at each of the four corners of the outer garment, one thread of each tassel to be deep blue. These tassels were to be for them a perpetual reminder of the law of God, and of their duty to keep it (see: Num 15:38–39 NIV). This was the hem which the poor woman touched, supposing there was some peculiar virtue in it. So the people of Gennesaret brought their sick to Christ for a similar purpose.[26]

Why do I include this woman in this study? Because she was marginalized by her condition, impoverished by her doctors, and had not Jesus intervened she would have very possibly ended without a home or means to survive. What this tells us is that our focus on the homeless should not be limited to those on the street, but must expand to those hanging on desperately to their homes before they lose them. If the church does not intervene in the lives of the poor and increasingly marginalized, many more sufferers will lose their homes.

Twenty-First Century Woman in the Crowd

Because Jesus intervened by putting this story of the hemorrhaging woman in his account, Luke shows Jesus demonstrating that there is no distinction among those whom God cares for, either rich or poor; one is no more important than the other. The way we treat potential and actual homeless women ought to be with respect for they too are God's children. "The hemorrhaging woman was considered ritually unclean and was excluded from social and religious relations. Jesus' healing of her removed the public stigma of her condition and smoothed the way for her reentry into social and religious life."[27]

This is actually what happened. Jesus' intervention saved her health, home, and means to survive. Three centuries later, Eusebius (cited earlier)

---

25. Eusebius, *Eusebius—The Church History*, 264–66.
26. Freeman and Chadwick, *Manners and Customs of the Bible*, 345.
27. *NIV Archaeological Study Bible*, 1574.

served as the Bishop in Caesarea Philippi, and he relates an insightful experience he had that shows just a reentry into social and religious life that Jesus' healing intervention into her life accomplished.

As Jesus was not afraid of the unclean, the destitute, the homeless, and those people who are turned away, the church does not need to fear them either. At one point we were all unclean in some manner, the first example being that we are sinful. We need and are continuously in need of a spiritual, emotional, and physical touch to make our situation whole again. The woman in the crowd had an issue. There are depths to one's issue. The issue can keep growing bigger and bigger, as with this woman in our passage, for twelve long years. I can imagine it started as a small issue that she thought would soon go away, but as the issue grew it began to affect other areas of her life. Like many of us, her physical issue led to an emotional issue, which led to a financial issue, which led to a spiritual issue. We all need someone to help us come back to a place of wholeness; that is what Jesus did, and we are also to help set the captive free, restore liberty to the oppressed and recover sight to the blind, by proclaiming his good news (physically, mentally, spiritually).

Let's look again at the woman in the crowd. Before Jesus intervened, she did not even have a name. She was unclean, struggling, outcast, and invisible. We spoke earlier of the homeless woman being classified as the "invisible." This invisibility simply means "less visible," causing her to go unnoticed. This is how the woman in the crowd lived her life, wishing to be recognized. As we saw with Hagar, when the angel of the Lord spoke to her and called her by name, she began to listen, believing the Lord met her where she was. There are women today who are living with the issue of an identity crisis and are only known by their issue. When Jesus responded to the woman, he gave her an identity, "daughter," and Jesus, knowing she had little money left, declared, "Your faith has made you whole." Discussing with women during one of my journaling sessions at the homeless shelter, I asked one woman to describe "who you are." Her answer was "homeless." She stated her reason: "That's how I am identified by the housing staff." She was identified by her issue and not her name. This woman was concerned that she was not treated as important—it overshadowed the physical help she was receiving. There are numerous homeless women with spiritual, emotional, and physical issues who the enemy would like nothing more than to leave bankrupt and helpless.

The twelve-year blood issue had taken over the life of the woman in the crowd. This stole everything from her: money, wellness, status, friends, acceptance; her plight eventually may have taken her home. She lost contact with everyone because she was unclean (according to Levitical law). This is an indication of how a small issue, as it grows, affects other areas in our lives resulting in bigger issues. This also happens at times to some of us, when issues in our life grow and magnify. Focusing on the homeless and marginalized women, we see their issues tend to grow in other ways as well: hunger, danger, and depression. These and others have overtaken them until their issue(s) have become their identity. Just like the woman in the crowd, who I am sure had a name, was identified and reduced to the "woman with the issue of blood." So it is with the marginalized, being referred to as the "person on the street," "beggar," "poor," and, yes, "the homeless woman" who could not get past seeing herself important in the eyes of those who helped her.

Church's Interpretation

The purpose of the Gospel of Luke was to give a historical account that would provide a basis for a well-grounded Christian faith for those who had already been taught, and perhaps those with less understanding of the story of Jesus.[28] "For a long time, Luke was the most neglected of the gospels. But one could make a case that Luke is the most pluralistic of the gospels and therefore it is tailor-made for the modern world."[29] Some argue that Luke is intending to defend the faithfulness of God's promise,[30] that the children of the promise are counted as offspring,[31] "while defending the inclusion of Gentiles and the rise of the new Christian community."[32] Luke's Gospel then is a call to everyone regardless of social class, or moral status. Christ is "the great friend of sinners" (Luke 7:34; 9:57–62; 18:9–14 NIV).[33]

---

28. Marshall, *Gospel of Luke*, 40.

29. Bock, *Luke*, 16.

30. Bock, *Luke*, 20.

31. This means that it is not the children of the flesh who are the children of God, but the children of the promise are counted as offspring (Rom 9:8).

32. Bock, *Luke*, 21.

33. Packer et al., *ESV Global Study Bible*, 1416.

Theme of Luke

The theme of this gospel is Jesus, the son of man who came "to seek and to save the lost" (Luke 19:10 NIV). Luke the physician wrote to his friend Theophilus to assure him that what he had heard was true, in that God fulfilled his purposes in the life and ministry of Jesus. Luke wrote from an unknown location about AD 70 to 75. Luke was a physician (Col 4:14 NIV) and traveled with Paul on parts of his missionary journey (Acts 16:10–17; 20:5–21:18; 27:1—28:16 NIV). It seems likely that Luke was a Gentile, and there is debate as to whether he was pure Gentile or non-Jewish Semite. In any case, he probably had religious contact with Judaism before coming to Christ.[34] The purpose of this gospel is stated in the prologue: "To write an orderly account for you, most excellent Theophilus, that you may have certainty concerning the things you have been taught" (1:3–4).

---

34. Bock, *Luke 1:1–9:50*, 7.

He is likely to be a medical doctor, possibly from Antioch of Syria, who is not Jewish, though whether he is Syrian or a Greco-Roman is not clear. The tradition also indicates that he lived a long life.

6

Summary of What We Learned in This Study

Wilma Faye Mathis

T HERE IS A CORRELATION between homelessness and suffering. We witness this with both Ruth and Hagar: poverty, grief, loss, emptiness, danger. Ruth was a Moabite. She was brought up a pagan in a culture hostile to the Israelites. She married an Israelite and he died, "then both Mahlon and Chilion also died" (Ruth 1:5 NIV). Ruth had to glean for a living and asked her mother-in-law, Naomi, to "please let me go to the field and glean among the ears of grain following one in whose eyes I may find favor" (Ruth 2:2 NIV). Because of the danger of being a foreigner, Boaz "ordered the servants not to touch you" (2:9).

Hagar is an Egyptian handmaiden: "Abram's wife Sarai took Hagar the Egyptian" (Gen 16:3 NIV). When Hagar discovers she is pregnant, Sarai "her mistress was insignificant in her sight." So "Sarai treated her harshly, and she fled from her presence" (16:4, 6). Hagar was cast out and "departed and wandered about in the wilderness of Beersheba" (21:14).

Suffering will either drive people to God or away from God. So, it is in our passage and in the lives of homeless women, illness, suffering, and life challenges can either drive homeless women to God or away from God. People tend to take desperate measures when their issues become unbearable, but we want people to be driven to God. The woman in the crowd found herself pressing through the crowd. Once coming into contact with Jesus, she hears Jesus say to her, "Daughter, your faith has made you well" (Luke 8:48 NIV). As Jesus did, we should desire those we come in contact with to leave well, or with hopes that it will be well. There are lessons to be learned through Jesus' responses. First, whenever approached by a homeless woman, we ought to respond with affection and tenderness. Using his example can help drive them to God. The woman in the crowd knew that her only hope was Jesus. If she could only touch, not him, but the "hem of his garment," if she had enough faith she would be made whole. Second, whenever we are among homeless women, we should leave an impact. There needs to be a residue that lingers in their minds: a scripture that was shared, comforting words, food, clothes, even money, that will bring them to a place where they desire to reach out and call, connect, and come back for more encouragement.

Further, as we see with Jesus, an interruption cannot always be viewed as annoying. This speaks volumes and allows us to recognize that Christians and churches today cannot avoid interruption. Jesus was often interrupted as we see in our passage of the woman in the crowd. He longs to restore the homeless, the poor, and widows but needs our hands and feet to show compassion, and to offer a better way. After all, we are representatives of Jesus among the homeless. He stopped to engage with the woman in the crowd, someone on the opposite end of the social spectrum, and called her "daughter." This may call for us to pause at the touch of a homeless woman, and we too can engage by calling her "friend" and address the need by journaling with her. When someone is pulling on the strings of our hearts, our response can help to bring rest: "Just as our bodies are what people see of us, so the church is what people see of Christ. As our bodies put our will into visible action, so Christ puts his will into visible action through the church."[1]

Whenever we look at someone worse off than we, the idea that this person could have been me should prompt us to respond. Jesus said, "Someone touched me" (Luke 8:46). He not only felt her touch but also responded. The heart of Jesus was for the poor and needy. "Throughout Luke, we then see the social and cultural reversals that take place as insiders are unconcerned about who Jesus is and what he is doing while outsiders are drawn to and understand Jesus."[2] Many of us are at different places in our lives regarding what we can do, but whatever it is, may we feel the need of others and then respond. To the person who is without, it can mean a world of difference to them. The global message of Luke for today can be summed up: "This is who God is. In Christ, the Friend of sinners, God is attracted to those who feel least attractive. The grace of the gospel qualifies those who feel most unqualified."[3]

1. Piper, "Christ in Combat," para. 8.
2. Packer et al., *ESV Global Study Bible*, 1415.
3. Packer et al., *ESV Global Study Bible*, 1416.

Successful Strategies of Christian Ministers to the Marginalized

7

Building Christian Community
for the Homeless

Jeanne C. DeFazio

I AM HONORED TO BE asked by Dr. Wilma Faye Mathis to contribute a chapter to her book about my work with the homeless. In the midst of an ongoing pandemic and a precarious economy, the homeless population is a major concern:

> 552,830 Americans are homeless and needlessly suffering tonight.1 in every 588 Americans is homeless. 194,467 people will sleep on the street across the USA tonight (HUD 2018).The ten states with the highest homeless rates account for 55% of the homeless population—CA, NY, FL, TX, WA, MA, OR, PA, IL, CO.18% are chronically homeless (HUD 2018).7% are unaccompanied youth under 25 (HUD 2018).7% are veterans (HUD 2018).[1]

My former boss Michael P. Grace II sponsored a homeless meeting that I organized in New York City from 1989 to 1995. I am highlighting this ministry to model Christian community as an effective strategy to help the homeless.

> The outreach was held at a McDonald's Restaurant in New York's Broadway theater district for anyone who needed a meal, prayer, or spiritual encouragement. Due to the growth of these ministries, the venue was changed to the third floor of the McDonald's Restaurant on 58th Street and Third Avenue. I purchased meal tickets from McDonald's which were distributed free to all who attended the monthly meeting. Pastor Robert Reith of Media Fellowship International encouraged this group with Scripture . . . . The culturally diverse attendees worshipped God in song

1. "Facts About Homelessness 2022," lines 1–8.

and testified of his grace. An unusual community developed; it included friends of Mr. Grace from society and the business world as well as homeless people from the West 51st Street Baptist Mission . . . .This event made a huge difference in my life . . . .This Christian community was novel in that it broke down social barriers and brought people from various walks of life together to worship Jesus. At these meetings, friendships developed between those who had previously felt uncomfortable within the traditional churches. The homeless no longer felt isolated. The hearts of those who attended the meetings felt the presence and love of God that was developing in the Christian community.[2]

In *Redeeming the Screens*, author and Ambassador of Prayer, April Shenandoah, describes a powerful move of the Holy Spirit through the teaching of the Word in one of those meetings:

During one evening at a McDonald's meeting, a small elderly man stood up to share. I do not know if he was homeless or just down on his luck, but I do know that I will never forget him. As he reached into his pocket and pulled out a small Bible, he spoke words filled with faith and such conviction that my spirit leaped for joy. His soft-spoken passion raised my faith when he told us not to look to people for anything, but to trust God for every need. This man was rich in my eyes. That is what these meetings were all about: being inspired and led by the Holy Spirit.[3]

This man was homeless and his trust in God's word impacted the entire community. He slept on the street and had very few teeth but when he preached, the Holy Spirit moved through him. In Matt 18:20 (KJV) Jesus promised: "For where two or three are gathered together in my name, there am I in the midst of them." The presence of the Holy Spirit was so great in our monthly meetings that everyone felt loved and accepted. Homeless Vietnam Veterans suffering from Post Traumatic Stress Disorder and nerve damage caused by Agent Orange (chemical warfare) attended regularly. Despite the trauma of psychological and physical illness, these wounded warriors felt at home in our meeting. They loved leading praise and worship and preaching to the community. The meetings were filmed and distributed by Mr. Grace among his peers. All the homeless enjoyed being viewed by an

2. DeFazio and Lathrop, *Creative Ways*, 7–8.

3. DeFazio and Spencer, *Redeeming the Screens*, 101–02; Spencers, *Christian Egalitarian Leadership*, 122.

extended community leading us all in prayer, praise and worship. Some of them were amazing preachers.

One homeless veteran who always had a kind word for everyone was noticeably absent at a monthly meeting. A woman asked me if I knew his next of kin so that the City of New York could notify them of his death. I did not. I was sad to lose such a wonderful Christian friend. I am grateful that our community provided him with Christian love, fellowship, and support. I feel certain that I will see him in heaven one day and that he is there praying for me now.

Our community provided the homeless with a place to come out of the cold at night, a meal, worship, prayer, scriptural support and warm fellowship. Our homeless veterans cared for everyone who attended as if it was a sacred commitment.

Vietnam Veteran Bruce McDaniel explains:

> In combat situations, I was aware of a strong ethic within the military that we take care of each other. We do not abandon wounded comrades on the battlefield. We do not leave our dead behind. It was a sacred commitment that we did not even question.[4]

The McDonald's monthly community was popular with the homeless because we bonded as Christian brothers and sisters. The homeless would update us on their lives as we ate burgers and fries together. We caught up with each other discussing the highs and lows of the previous month. We prayed for each other, sharing prayer requests and praise reports. Members of local churches attended the meeting regularly. They befriended the homeless and brought them into church communities where they were helped out of isolation and provided with support to rebuild their lives.

> There are many local church assistance programs for veterans, with churches running the gamut on the services that they provide for those in need. Some of the programs that are provided to help veterans include providing hot meals, having food pantries, giving homeless veterans a place to stay, and more. The programs are free of charge and open to anyone who needs the assistance. Most church programs provide the assistance year round, while some may only offer homeless shelter services during temperature extremes or when there is bad weather. Most local church programs

4. DeFazio, *Specialist Fourth Class*, 17.

do not use a strict eligibility process, which makes it easier for many people to obtain the help they need.[5]

Heb 13:2 reminds us: "Do not forget to show hospitality to strangers, for by doing so some people have shown hospitality to angels without knowing it" (NIV). There was an angelic presence in many of the homeless I served. I worked with Mother Teresa in Calcutta in 1987 and 1989 and volunteered in her Bronx, New York site in the early 1990s. She explained that there are many gifts that the poor give us as we serve them. Mother Teresa understood that we meet Jesus face-to-face when we help those who have nothing and nobody wants anything to do with. Many times I looked into the eyes of the homeless and saw Jesus smiling back at me. He speaks into our hearts in such a powerful way when we help the poor.

I asked friends to contribute their experiences of either being homeless or working with the marginalized to encourage others:

Tina Fuller:

> Many years ago there was a group of homeless people where I lived in Waltham, Massachusettes. They stayed in a place close to my house under the bridge. There were men and women. I came to know all of them. There was one whose name was Ron. I recently found out that he was burned up in a fire on Brown Street in my town. Ron and all of the group would come to my house and I would feed them and give them clothes. They would come to my house if they needed to open up cans. Debbie, one of the girls, died first. I took Ron to church so I could talk to him about the Lord. They were nice people who came from decent families but had bad breaks. Some of them had jobs but alcohol was a better friend than their own family so they would quit. They came and knocked on my door. My kids were not afraid. They were nice to my children. Over time the police made them leave but some of them would still stop by and ask for things. I tell my children never let them in when I am not home but if they need something let them have it. They were never rude. When I wasn't home they wouldn't ask. They would just leave. Thank God my kids learned something from that experience. And I did too.[6]

Pastor Mel Novak:

---

5. "Local Church Assistance Programs for Veterans," paras. 2–3.

6. Tina Fuller, interview by email, Jul 11, 2022.

I have ministered in the Skid Row Missions and some of the worst prisons all over the country for 39 years. I have done over 10,000 services and the Holy Spirit has brought in hundreds of thousands of souls behind enemy lines. I praise God that He has kept me in ministry for 39 years. On March 27, my anniversary started at the Union Rescue Mission where I was invited as "a guest celebrity" for Easter Sunrise Service. God had a plan (Jer 29:11–13) He gave me the supernatural strength and divine energy to do over 10,000 services in the devil's territory and the Holy Spirit (John 6:44) drew some 500,000 into the Kingdom. I give Him the honor, worship and glory.[7]

Aaron Ezra Mann

In the early to mid 1980s I assisted Evangelist Ada Schwartz who was ministering in the small chapel at the well-known Presbyterian Church in Hollywood, California. The Hollywood Presbyterian Church was the home to celebrity Pastor Lloyd Ogilvie, who later served as chaplain to the U.S. Senate. These meetings attracted an assortment of homeless, marginalized individuals from the neighborhood. One such homeless man, Mike, had graciously volunteered to play an old upright piano during worship and played like a true professional. Mike was wonderful! The crowd was quite "eclectic" with members of Hell's Angels, prostitutes, streetwalkers, drug users, etc. All were blessed by the outpouring of the Holy Spirit who were drawn in through the heartfelt praise and worship; not to mention the giftings of Ada Schwartz. Many received Jesus as their Lord and Savior at those services. A very kind, likable man by the name of Jimmy and benefactor to Ada, strummed an anointed guitar and often accompanied her. Jimmy also provided various snacks for everyone with leftovers always given to Mike. After serving under Ada's ministry a number of years, the Lord blessed me with my own ministry at His House Ministries. The meetings were held at the Beverly Hills home of a former child movie star from Japan, who later became a Hollywood movie producer. In his unique, loving style the Lord brought some of the same "eclectic" people from years earlier at the Hollywood Presbyterian Church to His House. Truly amazing! Once again the precious Holy Spirit was at work blessing us. Many were delivered and set free. . . but this time in Beverly Hills.[8]

---

7. Mel Novak Official Website, paras. 3–4.

8. Aaron Ezra Mann, interview by email, Jul 12, 2022

Charlene Eber:

I have retired from producing film and television in Hollywood and moved to Palm Desert. There are a lot of homeless people here in the desert. In my former capacity as co-founder and secretary of World Alliance for Peace, I made certain that a homeless program was financially subsidized through the foundation. In the desert I took a hands-on approach to the homeless. I befriended the homeless at church outreaches specifically designed to meet their needs. I showed love as well as prayed for them. During the lockdown churches are not open so it has been harder to continue outreaching with the homeless. We all need to give what we can and pray for the homeless to be safe from exposure to the coronavirus.[9]

Jozy Pollock:

I began to volunteer in prison ministry. I loved to exhort and encourage the inmates by sharing God's word and explaining that Bible heroes were imprisoned while continuing to fulfill God's call on their lives. I had married a famous magician and had had a lot of magical times. After I came to the Lord, the magical part of my life was introducing prisoners to Jesus, who supernaturally transforms the lives of those who receive him as Lord and Savior. The inmates were encouraged by this message of hope and many prayed the sinner's prayer. They claimed I had a direct line to God and sought me out at the Los Angeles County Jail. I never had children and I loved the inmates as if they were my children. People in jail do not understand that God loves them. They need Jesus love.[10]

Linda Lockhart

I volunteer with an outreach to the homeless on the Boston Common through a local church. There was a time in my life that God called me to live among the homeless. Actually it was a men's shelter in Atlanta where they had a room for women. Some of the men in the shelter were recovering addicts; it was very dark downstairs where the men slept. The women stayed upstairs in the entrance area of the building.

They slept in chairs along with their children. I remained there for a month or two. We had to leave each morning from 4 to 4:30 to go to a day shelter. We waited outside for the day shelter to open. They fed us breakfast and lunch. After lunch we were bussed

9. DeFazio, *Commission*, 28–29.

10. DeFazio and Spencer, *Redeeming The Screens*, 68.

back to the men's shelter. I was allowed to go into a bathroom on the side of the room where we slept to wash up. While living in the shelter, I prayed with and for the women I lived with. I understood the hardship of the homeless life. It gave me compassion. I don't turn and look the other way when I see the homeless without saying a prayer or offering a kind word or food after my experience. I was robbed while living in a shelter so I had to trust God completely for a place to live, food to eat, clothes to wear and for a place to shower. The Lord is my shepherd. He brought me through that valley. I feel more gratitude for what I have after that experience. Thanking God daily for a roof over my head, enough money for rent, utilities, food and healthcare. Jehovah Jireh is my provider. His grace is sufficient for me.[11]

Fred Hutchings:

I have experience with homelessness. In fact, I have been homeless. Some 30 years ago, I burned out from Insurance Sales. That is how I ended up in Fitchburg. Living in a homeless shelter, in the Fitchburg Public Library, I met the woman that was to become my son's mother. When at times I wish I had become a financial success and never become homeless, I think of my son, Alex. He is the best most precious event in my life. I would change nothing. I think God is a Good God. He showed me the way out. I would change nothing. May the Father God of the Universe Watch Over You. May Jesus' Mercy Touch All of Our Hearts. May the Holy Spirit be Your constant companion.[12]

Larry Abernathy:

The Cathedral of Love Outreach Ministries to the homeless and needy in the desert is based on Matt 25:34, 40. As our Lord Jesus said. And upon Isa 58:6, 8. For 35 years this miracle has and is happening. Our Lord Jesus shows us His heart, just before He and His Apostles would eat the Passover, and He would then give Himself up to be Crucified. Matt 25, Jesus shows the Church His heart for the homeless, and needy, that we have been called to meet the needs of all of His people. "In that you have done it unto one of the least of these my brethren you have done it unto Me" Matt 25:40 (NIV). God's people of love and prayer do what Isa 58:6, 7, "Is it not to deal thy bread to the hungry, and that thou bring the poor that are cast out to thy house?"... vs. 8, concludes in great promise,

11. Linda Lockhart, interview by email, Jul 13, 2022
12. Fred Hutchings. interview by email, Jul 17, 2022.

" and thy righteousness shall go before thee, the glory of the Lord shall be thy reward" (NIV). All praise be unto our God.[13]

Louise Maguire:

I was employed as a clinician in a juvenile detention center providing direct services, including individual and group psychotherapy as well as case management services. The majority of my clients were Hispanics who entered this country from Central America. They were primarily monolingual and spoke Spanish only. The majority of my clients escaped in search of reunifying with family members. There were others who traveled through Mexico trafficking drugs for the cartels. Most clients were of low socioeconomic status. The majority were held on felony crimes such as murder, aggravated assault, sexual assault, and burglary; therefore, the majority of these clients were ineligible for amnesty. The clients were males between the ages of eleven and seventeen. The majority were later incarcerated by the Department of Juvenile Justice and incarcerated in jail at eighteen years of age. I never interfaced with family members to witness any family reunification. Unfortunately, I was also totally unsuccessful with finding any family members, despite numerous inquiries. The majority of these youth seldom expressed remorse for their alleged criminal behavior. I observed numerous assaults by these youth on both staff and peers. This detention facility was frequently on lockdown due to episodes of violent behavior. There were no incidents of these youth being transferred to community-based placements; these youth were then sent to the Department of Corrections upon discharge to either await trial or serve sentences. It is very sad to state that their future outcomes were rather bleak despite their very tender ages. I developed trust by providing empathy, rapport, and positive, strength-based communication. I expressed social disapproval of all inappropriate behaviors, especially racial slurs. I promoted appropriate behavior with individual counseling to encourage assertive communication and provided very strong verbal praise. I practiced modeling appropriate behavior without engaging in either physical conflicts and/or making verbal threats. I encouraged practicing alternate coping skills with strength-based strategies. I verbalized the very vital importance that both following the rules and following their individualized service plans would result in a possible transition to a community-based placement. I constantly encouraged the

13. Larry Abernathy, interview by email, Jul 15, 2022.

clients to follow their service plans to graduate to a lower level of care. I encouraged the youth to use their words to verbalize their anger without engaging in physical conflict. I provided both ethnic and favorite foods of choice, such as tacos, pupusas, fried chicken chips, and salsa, Takis, potato chips, cupcakes, and cookies. I celebrated both holidays and birthdays with hands-on activities and food. I consistently acknowledged both the educational and vocational opportunities that are abundant in this very wonderful country. I would encourage them to follow rules and study hard to take advantage of these opportunities. I repeated the following: "Please follow the rules of this facility." "We follow rules and ensure success." "There are also infinite opportunities awaiting you." "By modeling appropriate behavior and following the house rules, you will be able to transition to a community-based facility." "Following the rules also assures graduation of this transition successfully." I had a wonderful Christian supervisor and I was allowed to share my faith when appropriate. My prayer life skyrocketed while working with these clients. At the onset, the clients treated me with contempt and hostility; at the end of the term of my service, they thanked me for caring and food incentives. In spite of the grim realities of their life circumstances, we bonded as clinician and clients in a positive way.[14]

Gemma Wenger:

As a young 21-year-old, my desire to serve God outweighed any other aspirations in my life. I couldn't get enough of Him, nor could I get enough of serving Him. I started ministering in the prisons and from there God opened the door to minister on the streets of Skid Row. Skid Row in Los Angeles, California is the mothership of homeless encampments, addiction, drugs, prostitution, mental illness, and crime. As a bright-eyed faith-filled minister, I knew the power of God could change the lives of these very needy and hurting people. All I had to do was preach the word of God to them and pray for them. The Lord would do the rest.

As a minister to the homeless, there is no "how to" booklet or "things you should know" pamphlet preparing you for what to expect! I have only first-hand experience for over 30 years of consistent ministry to these marginalized people. Through my own personal experiences, I now understand the homeless population, and the unique characteristics belonging to that subgroup.

14. DeFazio, *Finding A Better Way*, 14–16.

When I first started my homeless ministry, I thought that those in need would immediately come to the altar, and in turn, get the help that was being offered to them. What I realized is that was not the case. The offer of a program to get the homeless off the streets was available, but those who qualified did not want to enroll. They participated in the church service, listened to the sermon required to get a meal, and then headed back onto the street for the same life that they had just left. They had no intention of changing anything, let alone their lifestyle. To get into a program one has to leave the drugs, the alcohol, the established ways on the streets and embrace a new walk. That transition takes discipline and commitment. Most do not have that.

One experience was very enlightening in broadening my understanding of the mindset of the homeless. For about ten years I had been ministering at the Salvation Army to a homeless Black gentleman with beautiful blue eyes. My nickname for him was "Blue Eyes". At times I would even call him up at the end of the service to pray over him. Every week for a good ten years, I would see him sitting in the audience. One day he came up to me and said that he just asked Jesus in his heart. Though happy to hear that, I was flabbergasted as I thought he had already committed himself to the Lord as he sat listening to my sermons for the past ten years! It made me realize that it is only the power of God that can touch people's hearts and cause them to turn from a life of sin to the living God. These people are blinded to the fact that they are living in squalor, and without submitting to the power of God, have no strength to change their lives. He did not receive the full revelation of the presence of God until God took the blinders off of his eyes, and he could see clearly. I also realized that it took time for the seed of the word of God planted in his heart to grow and bear tangible fruit.

Homelessness is a spiritual battle. I was ministering to a lady at my church service located in Beverly Hills at the time who was homeless. I let her stay with me in my apartment one night. The next morning a demonic violent angry spirit took control of her, and she literally grabbed the necklaces with cross pendants from around my neck and pulled them off and broke them. I was in tears and extremely fearful. I managed to secure for her a hotel room in downtown Los Angeles through a Christian friend, only to find that she was asked to leave because she was violently banging her head on the wall of the room and creating a massive hole. Even when she was given a place to stay, she was unable to maintain it due to the spiritual strongholds that were controlling her life. The issue wasn't housing availability or even money for that matter; the issue was a spiritual bondage from which she needed to be delivered.

A few weeks later she again showed up at my church. When it was over, she followed me to my car and tried to get violent. My mother and a fellow minister distracted her so I could safely leave. When I drove away, the radio show that was playing was *Focus on the Family* with James Dobson. He was talking to a woman whose son was deemed the second most violent child in America. I immediately saw a connection between the homeless woman and this child. They both had a demon that manifested itself in extremely violent behavior. Because of the timing of the radio show and my experience with that exact same type of evil spirit, it was reassuring to know that God knew what I was going through with this woman, and he was there to help me understand her spiritual needs on a whole new level. There is an answer to homelessness, but only Jesus' power can deliver from demonic oppression. The devil was trying to steal the homeless woman's blessing of a permanent place to stay at every turn.

There was a very memorable homeless gentleman who would consistently come to my meetings when they were held in Santa Monica. His name was "Clay". He grew up in foster homes and at a very young age began engaging in illicit activities and ended up in juvenile hall. His lifestyle was living on the streets between Washington and 10th Streets behind a church. The uncanny characteristic about Clay was that he could prophesy. When he prophesied, he literally "read your mail". God spoke through him miraculously. It was truly astounding. When I was at my lowest, and I had a great need to hear the word of the Lord, God would use Clay to speak powerful words of encouragement that literally strengthened my body and my spirit to continue on my walk.

One morning, I had a very interesting encounter as I was getting my car serviced at the BMW dealership in Santa Monica. As I was waiting, who should come walking down the street but Clay. I said, "Hello," only to realize that he reeked of alcohol. He had such a great call on his life, but he was not able to overcome the addiction that controlled him. I was also told that Clay had once been offered an apartment in which to live that he readily accepted, only to be removed due to his violent temper and lack of anger management. I know Clay is bitter at the world and bitter at his circumstances, but he is not willing to overcome the anger and addiction that possesses him and robs him of his blessings. People get mad at God, without realizing that it is their own lifestyle, and the sin in their lives that is stealing the rewards God wants to give them.

Another profound experience which gave me further revelation on the plight of the homeless occurred when I was at the Salvation Army ministering. I brought my cameras to film for my television show "Beauty for Ashes". When the homeless who were seated, saw the cameras, they immediately hollered in unison, "Get that camera out of here!" Instead of being happy that the service would be filmed for television and that this was an opportunity to glorify God, they were irate. I realized that most of them did not want to be found due to warrants out for their arrest, illicit activities, and lack of taking responsibility for their actions in the past. We aren't dealing with people who don't have money; we are dealing with people who need deliverance from sin and demonic oppression in their lives. We are dealing with people who have become comfortable in their lifestyle and are not willing to put forth the effort to make the necessary changes in order to become upstanding citizens who are able to live in a home instead of on the streets.

I have always said that the issue with the homeless is not that they don't have money or that they don't have a home. There is a plethora of money earmarked to support the homeless who want to get off the streets. Many times mental illness is involved that prevents people from getting and keeping a job; many times people don't want to work and would rather live off of other people or the government; many times drug and alcohol addiction has laid the path for decreased mental capacity and the inability to deal with problems in an appropriate manner; many times the lifestyle on the streets consisting of prostitution, pimping, and crime has overtaken people's hearts, and they refuse to jeopardize an illegitimate source of income to turn to an honest way of making money; and many times living on the street has become easy and comfortable. No one is there to tell you what to do or discipline you. You can do whatever you want. Sometimes deep trauma and abuse have caused people to follow a lifestyle on the street, and the only possibility of deliverance is through the healing power of the Lord Jesus Christ! Many who were once incarcerated as well as veterans suffering from Post-Traumatic Stress Disorder can be found on the streets. Through faith, God can heal any situation or circumstance, but people have to be willing to follow God and leave the past behind. They have to possess the fortitude to press forward, endure and never give up until they achieve victory. Many are unable to do that and continue to wallow in poverty and lack.

People think that the homeless are typical people who have lost their jobs and couldn't pay their rent. There are some like that, but they are quickly assimilated into a program and given the support they need to access society in a positive way. For the rest, the only hope is surrendering their life to the Lord, calling on the power of the Holy Spirit, resisting the devil and his temptations, and submitting to God's will and God's plan. Being an overcomer, will take all the strength a person can conjure up within themselves to conquer the temptation. Some are not willing to pay the price to be delivered from darkness and choose to continue in sin just as Clay did when he wouldn't give up the alcohol or the deep seeded anger and unforgiveness within him.

Homeless families and children are becoming increasingly more prevalent on the streets of skid row. Unless the spiritual cycle of oppression is destroyed by the power of God, the next generation will perpetuate the curse of poverty, sin, addiction, mental illness, and lack. Money is not the answer, only the delivering power of the Lord Jesus Christ can bring a change to the hearts of the hurting and hopeless living on the streets.

I noticed a very unusual occurrence each month when I went to minister to the homeless at the Salvation Army. When I came to minister on the first Monday and the first Saturday of the month, the attendance was low. When I arrived on the third Monday of the month, the chapel auditorium was packed. I subsequently learned that General Relief checks were given at the beginning of the month and were spent by the end of the month. It was at that time at the end of the month that the homeless needed the support of the various missions to supplement their income in order to eat. Because the homeless had a need, they showed up to the church service which they were required to attend, prior to eating. When they had the money, they would eat at places of their choosing or purchase drugs and alcohol. When the money ran out, then they would show up at the doors of the church. Having no money would actually lead the homeless to church to receive the word of the Lord.

Living off a government wage will keep you poor. The amount is not enough to live on, but it is just enough to prevent you from working 40 hours a week at a job that pays only a tiny bit more than you are already making by not working. Having to work a fulltime job for such a small increase in salary is not seen as desirable even to the homeless. They would rather not work at all for a smaller amount of money than work fulltime and only receive a moderate increase in pay. Someone once said that the difference between a living wage and the poverty line is only a couple hundred dollars. That small increase in money makes all the difference in the world. The impetus to leave the support of the government and begin a new life can only come from the power of the Lord Jesus Christ. It is only the Lord that strengthens the heart of each individual to release the old and make the decision to lead a new life in the way that God intended for his children.[15]

Conclusion

In *Creative Ways*, I explained:

> By 1986, I was working as Mr. Grace's executive assistant in both New York City and Los Angeles. I had a hectic schedule with great responsibilities administering Mr. Grace's legal, banking, social, and charitable activities. I was reluctant to take on any more responsibility, but Mr. Grace directed me to organize his World Alliance for Peace New York City Bible study.[16]

I always understood what Jesus meant when he said: ""The King will reply, 'Truly I tell you, whatever you did for one of the least of these brothers and sisters of mine, you did for me. (Matt 25:40, NIV). But I had no revelation knowledge of this Scripture until I spent 1989 to 1995 organizing the McDonald's outreach. "And what I got was the opportunity to work incredibly hard—along with a real and utterly spiritual sense of mission."[17]

I currently reside in a middle-class residential area of Davis, California. Since the pandemic, more homeless people sleep in the park across the street from my home and in their cars in the parking lots of the local grocery stores. I began this chapter referencing statistics that identify California as the state with the highest homeless population in the United States. I agree with former California Governor Jerry Brown's concern:

> "We have to restore power to the family, to the neighborhood, and the community with a non-market principle, a principle of equality, of charity, of let's-take-care-of-one-another. That's the creative challenge."[18]

---

15. Gemma Wenger, interview by email, Aug 9, 2022.

16. DeFazio and Lathrop, *Creative Ways*, 7.

17. Wiles, "U.S. Sen. Rockefeller Delivers Farewell Speech," para 4.

18. Brown, "We Have to Restore Power."

Before COVID, I volunteered with the local rotating homeless shelter. Since I am caring for my ninety-three-year-old mom during the pandemic, I donate what I can to the churches that participate in the shelter program because I cannot volunteer in person.

> My life has been transformed by Christian service and membership in Christian community. I hope and pray that you too have already, or will, experience the joy and love of Jesus, and grow in the knowledge of his grace through similar involvement in active Christian community.[19]

---

19. DeFazio and Lathrop, *Creative Ways*, 26.

8

The Hosanna Foundation

Martha Reyes

THE HOSANNA FOUNDATION IS a California nonprofit organization that helps hundreds of minority individuals and their families in areas of mental health. We have fifteen bilingual psychologists and mental health care professionals from the US, Mexico, Guatemala, Venezuela, Colombia, and El Salvador, offering pro bono or low-cost counseling, group sessions, and seminars.

We at the Hosanna Foundation firmly believe that by taking care of social, emotional, and psychological needs and giving tools to overcome personal hardships and adversities, we can provide urgently needed mechanisms for individuals and society. By reducing addiction, domestic violence, crime, broken homes, and abandonment, and by improving the overall stability of family life and personal wellness, it will be possible to positively impact the future well-being and prosperity of generations to come.

The Hosanna Foundation has offered frequent workshops at the Heffernan Memorial in Calexico, at CEDIM Center in Corona, California (Centro De Salud Integral Para La Mujer), and at different meeting halls, convention centers, schools, and churches in cities across the US. These seminars have focused on marriage, family life, parenting, domestic violence, depression, grief, family reunification, migration, traumatic experiences, addictions, and many other needs.

Our Mission: Changing Lives and Destinies

Over the years, after reaching out to hundreds of disadvantaged individuals and communities in a multicultural and multilingual setting, offering our educational services and counseling and networking with the local community and faith-based projects, the testimonies of impacted lives have been numerous. Placing extreme value on community and fellowship and fostering emotional, psychological, and spiritual well-being also aids in interconnecting people of diverse ethnic origins but with similar experiences and social needs. All this will help promote healing relationships and empower the weakened.

Attending the Needs of Today's Youth

The social life and pressures that teens face today are simply overwhelming. Our youth services and programs are designed to help youth feel relevant, safe, and engaged. Young people get to share their needs during private counseling sessions or group sessions. These group sessions are also an opportunity to interact, mingle, and befriend others of similar backgrounds, experiences, and purposes.

The Value of Helping Others

The value of helping others is immeasurable in that it connects us to God and the noblest feelings of human beings. Acts of charity make us grow in empathy, love for others, and wisdom. They allow us to value the blessings and recognize perfection in God's time.

Building strong bonds between neighbors and a solid community foundation takes work. Our organization provides opportunities for people to become involved in the greater community and throughout the state. We interconnect with mutual needs and resources by serving our city and neighbors. Helping people requires an awakened and humble conscience to listen and learn. With great respect for our capabilities and virtues, we will act to help others as they need and ask for it. We ask our staff and volunteers to engage in acts of selfless giving and empathic care continually.

Ten Actions to Help Others

At our office we posted this sign:

1. Emotional support. Give your time and listen to someone who needs to talk about their experience or problem. Do it without judging, but be an active, empathic listener.

2. Look around. A plant that needs water, a lost puppy, a lonely older adult, an overwhelmed colleague, or someone in trouble. Come and say hello. See if it is suitable or better to withdraw.

3. At home, there are always actions to help others. Spend a few hours doing tasks others postpone that make life easier for everyone in your home.

4. Smile. Your smile is always a great help to others. Always seek to spread enthusiasm and love of life, even with strangers. Smiles can be contagious.

5. Correspond. You too have received help at another time. Never forget the one who extended your hand and remained attentive to any need you had.

6. Congratulate or acknowledge the good in each person, every job well done, especially if you have seen them go the extra mile, recognize them and encourage them.

7. Be kind to everyone. A gesture, the slightest action to help others all add to social welfare that benefits us all.

8. Be generous by paying for coffee for a homeless person. Offer to clothe those who do not have. Assist organizations that help so many people.

9. Pray. You don't need to go to a temple or say a prayer from memory. Just enter a quiet room or find a perfect spot. God listens in the depths of your heart. Ask for everyone, for the needs of each person, even those of your enemies.

10. Identify your gifts and what you are good at and offer them as a service to the community—for example, tutoring a child, conversing with the elderly, preparing food, and spending time with children.

Comforting the Suffering

One of the greatest works of mercy is the gift of comfort. To accompany our brothers and sisters in all moments, but especially in the most difficult ones, is to practice the behavior of Jesus. He sympathized with the pain of others and offered the joy of the gospel.

Pray for all the poor. When you pray for others, even if you do not know them personally, you stand in solidarity with them. We must all intercede before God for those who suffer poverty, marginalization, misery, and social inequalities.

"Remember the needy, for you are also needy; remember the poor, for you are too; no matter how much you swim in riches, you are dressed in rags of meat," said St. Augustine. All people are poor at some point, materially or spiritually. As Christians, it is necessary to always be by their side.

The Homeless

When we think of homelessness, we usually think of jobless adults with a mental illness, drug addiction, or impoverished by different social ills. But many children live in the streets, children of homeless adults, and migrant children sent to cross the border alone, without parents or caretakers.

It is estimated that around 120 million children live on the streets worldwide (30 million in Africa, 30 million in Asia, and 60 million in South America). In addition, these children are often victims of all kinds of abuse.

What is a street child?

They are minors who live (or survive) on the streets. They often grow up in public landfills, train stations, or under the bridges of large cities. Because of their conflicts with their families, these children are unwilling or unable to return home.

Why does a child live on the street?

There are several reasons a child decides to live on the street. The combination of family, economic, social, and political factors play an essential role in their situation, and it isn't easy to decisively pinpoint one or more causes.

However, children who have been asked say that family, poverty, abuse, or war, among other reasons, are often reasons to take to the streets.

What problems do children encounter on the street?

Growing up in a dangerous environment could make children easy prey of criminality, lawlessness, and prostitution.

As a result, some of their rights are frequently compromised:

Right to Food

Street children often do not have access to a healthy diet. Sometimes, they don't even have food because living on the streets, they have no way to produce it, nor do they have money to buy it. They eat what they sometimes find in other people's trash. When they have the opportunity to choose, they are inclined to unhealthy foods such as ice cream or cakes, so they are at risk of malnutrition. Growth problems and childhood diseases are also common among these children.

Right to Health Care

The health of children growing up on the streets is strongly compromised. They have no access to sanitary facilities and are often dirty and infested with lice. These children are exposed to diseases due to a lack of hygiene, and their health is often worrying. Without a family to take care of them, these minors must take care of themselves. In addition, street children frequently use cannabis and alcohol or inhale natural gas to escape reality. Unfortunately, these harsh living conditions negatively impact their physical and psychological development.

Right to Education

Street children are not educated. For this reason, they do not have the same opportunities as other children. They are prevented from finding employment and changing their situation because they cannot envision any future for themselves and because they cannot have vocational training.

Right to Non-discrimination

Seen as marginal, street youth are often victims of discrimination. Generally, adults have prejudices that stigmatize them and are often associated with the dangers of the streets. It is often difficult for these children to reintegrate into society.

What Can Be Done to Help Street Children?

To better understand children living and growing up on the streets, it is essential to involve them and put them in contact with critical institutions or people who seek to understand the structural causes of their situation.

In the US and other socially organized countries, government agencies and non-profit organizations are constantly looking for these children to find foster care alternatives in the community. The population generally resists walking around neighborhoods of homeless camps and shelters. But when volunteers approach these places, they can immediately spot the children living under undesirable conditions and are prompted to help. Separating children from their parents is complex, with severe emotional consequences. Mental health care professionals must assess each situation carefully and compassionately, and prioritize finding help for the entire family unit.

Between 2021 and 2022, over two hundred thousand homeless individuals, many with children, have crossed the US border illegally. Many more are expected to keep crossing the border. The traumas associated with migration include separation from loved ones, physical and sexual harm, and illnesses, and it will be a constant reminder of the need for organizations like ours. The Hosanna Foundation has provided hundreds of hours of counseling and assistance to families affected by all these social challenges.

9

Empowering the Practical Lives of Women through Transformational Journaling Exercises

Wilma Faye Mathis

T HE GOSPEL CAUSES A transformation in the lives of homeless women. As we have seen in our study, Scripture shows that ministry to the homeless is important. It is the churches' responsibility to make sure that such transformation is encouraged to happen. We are instructed to care for widows and orphans (including the homeless). The ingredient for acting in Christ's community is our calling (in order words what you are called to do is essential in the body of Christ and to our community and society).

During the spring of 2014, Boston community activist Sara Mitchell started an outreach initiative of journaling and art activities on Christian topics. Sara chose to journal because the Congregation Lion of Judah, with whom she was working at the time, does a chapel service at the Woods-Mullen Women's Shelter on Tuesdays, so she wanted her team of volunteers, of which I am one, to do something different. We did the first six weeks collectively with all five volunteers. The volunteers committed for only six weeks but all of us decided we wanted to continue. This resulted in dividing up into two teams. Each team had a leader. The teams rotated for three weeks in the women's shelter, and the fourth week was a collective meeting with both teams. We would debrief, discuss what was working and not, then come up with new ideas for the next month's journaling session. As Amanda Dillon notes,

> Bible Journaling is a trend of the past decade whereby readers make creative, visual interventions in their Bibles, using coloured pens and pencils, watercolors, stickers and stencils, highlighting

texts of particular resonance. Journaling, in its more conventional written forms, has long been recognised as a pathway to spiritual development. Significantly, Bible journaling is almost exclusively practiced by women and has a high level of interpersonal interaction attached to it, through open and mutual sharing of these creations, through various online social media fora.[1]

Since journaling plays a positive role in aiding recovery from drug addiction, biblical transformational journaling can also play positive roles in helping homeless women. Journaling provides hope and self-esteem, not only to exist but also to thrive and develop whole life patterns within these women.

While writing this book, I have been noticing many things happening in our world: a global pandemic, COVID-19, stay-at-home orders, joblessness, over eight hundred thousand COVID-related deaths alone in the United States, and many people displaced, including homeless women. Many of the homeless and those facing homelessness have taken to the streets. There is an intersection in Boston where Massachusetts Avenue and Melnea Cass Boulevard meet, and it is known as "Mass and Cass." This is the area where the women's shelter we were serving (pre-COVID) is located. "It is an area of Boston with a long history of serving the City's—and the region's—most vulnerable populations."[2] Boston has faced chronic homelessness for years.

Long before the COVID-19 pandemic upended life across the city, many Bostonians were already dealing with a public health tragedy: the convergence of mental and behavioral health, homelessness, and substance use disorder crises at the intersection of Mass Ave and Melnea Cass Blvd (Mass & Cass). "One thing is clear, Mass and Cass is ground zero for twin wars: the wars on people who use drugs and people experiencing homelessness. COVID-19 terminated the indoor ecosystem of services to people . . . It exposed massive inequality in the US in a way that was harder than ever to deny."[3]

This area often becomes a tent city. Wherever you go up and down Mass and Cass, all one can see are rows and rows of makeshift tents, as "camping tents line the sidewalks near the public homeless shelter for men on Southampton Street. One tent has the words 'Hated by Many—Loved

---

1. Dillon, "Bible Journaling as a Spiritual Aid," para 1.
2. "Policy and Advocacy—Melnea Cass / Mass. Ave. 2.0."
3. "Boston's 'Methadone Mile,'" paras. 2, 21–22.

by None' scrawled on it. Sidewalks are strewn with garbage, wet clothing, and discarded needles. People gather and roam. Many openly use drugs."[4]

4. "Jolicoeur, "This Doctor Has Spent Decades," para. 2.

This most recent version has been going on at least since spring 2021 and the latest news is that Boston Mayor Michelle Wu announced last week that the city plans to clear encampments in the area surrounding Massachusetts Avenue and Melnea Cass Boulevard no later than Jan 12 by connecting people living in tents to appropriate services, including supportive housing that is or will be made available in coming weeks.[5]

Many of the homeless are discouraged and not very hopeful that the city will provide safe housing: "From his perch on a broken desk chair outside his own tent, José, who asked GBH News not to use his last name, smoked a cigarette and watched the bins being loaded into big white vans. 'I don't want to stay here,' José told GBH News. 'But now I have no place to go.'"[6] And here is the perspective of a woman who feels the mandate of rushing to move people out is not helping: "Mercedes, who asked GBH News not to use her last name, ran back and forth from the van to her friend's tent, packing things into boxes in a frantic rush, saying, 'If this was really helping, people wouldn't be rushing out like this,' since 'people don't want to be forced out of here and into a shelter.'"[7] What this action really means is that with no permanent housing, unfortunately, people will eventually be back onto the streets.

Situations such as these increase the reason transformational journaling is needed. It can help to equip homeless women with an ability to

5. Lamb, "Wu Says Tents Will Be Cleared," para. 1.

6. Bedford, "'I Have No Place to Go,'" paras. 2–3.

7. Bedford, "'I Have No Place to Go,'" para. 17.

recognize and exercise their God-given purpose in every aspect of their lives: spiritually, mentally, and physically, while engaging the journaling process in a profound way with the biblical text at its foundation. Because of the unfortunate situations to which the homeless succumb, women are still living in homeless shelters and trying to survive. With that said, we will turn our attention to the practical aspect of how journaling has helped women we had the privilege to walk alongside.

We learned some amazing and not-so-amazing things about the women living in homeless shelters. Nonetheless, each of them left an imprint on our hearts. Their names are pseudonyms to protect their identity. We will begin with a woman who was instrumental to this ministry and loved.

Picture Chelsea, Massachusetts before its day begins to blossom. It's just after 9 a.m. in Bellingham Square. A woman in a pink sweatshirt, bent over at the waist, sways back and forth in the middle of McDonald's, pausing her drug-induced dance to zero in on a ketchup packet before lurching out the door. No one pays much attention; it's a common scene here in the heart of downtown Chelsea, a magnet for addicts, alcoholics, prostitutes, and the homeless. As workers hand burgers and fries across the counter at McDonald's, small-time dealers, huddling at the tables, pass heroin to customers and sell prescription pills out of Ziploc bags.[8]

Penny: this young woman who was not unlike the archetypical woman just described. She was actively using and had been in various recovery programs. However, she met a Christian outreach worker in Bellingham Square in Chelsea by the name of Ruben Rodrigues.[9] He directed her to Starlight Ministries and the South End Neighborhood Church in Boston.

We met Penny at this local church she had been attending while she lived at the shelter. As we got to know her and time went on, we noticed that journaling was a big part of her recovery. When asked if she thought a journaling group would be helpful at the shelter, she became very excited. Penny was an inspiration for the program. She has been a good promoter and has given us sound insight into the population we wanted to serve.

---

8. Johnston, "As Chelsea Begins to Blossom," paras. 1–3.

9. Johnston, "As Chelsea Begins to Blossom," para. 30.

One of the outreach workers is Ruben Rodriguez, a former drug addict turned missionary who first saw the need when he was handing out Bible tracts in the square. Soon he was bringing van loads of donated food from Trader Joe's, learning of people's woes as they stood in line for basil pesto sausages and Belgian endive. Now he talks to alcoholics and drug addicts about getting sober, accompanies people to court, and takes suicidal residents to the hospital.

When given $20 to buy whatever she wanted to enhance the journaling experience, she purchased tablecloths, candles, and provided music, as a way to break up the day and provide the women a sacred place of peace. Penny was the person who assisted in rounding up the women to come to the journaling sessions. She eventually obtained an apartment, worked at the shelter, and was pleased that we carried out her ideas while doing the journaling at this shelter.

Penny, in early recovery, could find no job and was inconsistent in anything she said she would do. However, with connection to the church and journaling, she had a change in understanding her faith, self-confidence, consistency, and helping others. She landed a job, had an improved relationship with her mother (who was keeping her children), and plans to attend the University of Massachusetts for a certificate in substance abuse treatment. She did much of the work herself but believes her outcome was enhanced by her connection with believers, the availability of Bible study at Starlight Ministries, South End Neighborhood Church, and the journaling activities.

Here are the perspectives of a few other women who stood out during our transformational journaling sessions and here are the stories we captured as we learned from these women who wanted more for their lives.

Ms. Ungrateful: A gentleman associated with Starlight Ministries who worked among the homeless shared with us about a homeless woman in the church where he is a ruling elder. This woman he described as a sinkhole for help. She was demanding and resentful, her attitude alienated everyone, she had phenomenal control issues, and never expressed any gratitude. When people tried helping her to get an apartment, or enter into various programs, she would repeatedly break the rules which in turn left her continually homeless. Ms. Ungrateful had a boyfriend that abused alcohol and her instability eventually helped destroy him. These types of situations are so disruptive that they can be a danger not only to themselves but to others. Nothing that was given to her could restore her status but transformation could. Steve Corbett explains that simply giving a person money is treating the symptoms rather than the underlying condition, which in turn increases the lack of self-discipline.[10] That is why the church needs to intervene for those on the streets and for those on the verge of homelessness before they end up on the streets. We can all run into homeless people and wonder, What do I do? This may sound strange, but in some cases "money does

10. Corbett, *When Helping Hurts*, 53.

more harm than good, and it would be better not to do anything at all than to give a handout."[11] For some, "a better—and far more costly—solution would be for your church to develop a relationship" with people who are homeless. A relationship says, "We are here to walk with you and to help you use your gifts and abilities to avoid being in this situation in the future. Let us into your life and let us work with you to determine the reason you are in this predicament."[12] Like Jesus, who while passing by, stopped for the woman in the crowd and offered her healing, we too can stop for the homeless, and offer them the good news of hope.

The Runner: Referenced earlier, she was the woman I asked to describe herself and who simply answered: "Homeless." She stated her reason, "That's how I am identified by the housing staff." She was identified by her issue and not her name. This woman was concerned that she was not treated as important—her homeless state had overshadowed the physical help she was receiving. She was not confident and referred to herself as someone with no real identity. Whatever someone called her became her identity (homeless, uneducated). This was an issue we saw that emerged through journaling. The Runner could not process how much help she was receiving, being unable to get past seeing herself as important in the eyes of those who were trying to help. However, she often talked about how she loved running and even attempted to run in the marathon. This was her niche, so while interacting with the Runner, we made sure this was part of our conversation. She always lit up and you could see the spark in her eyes. The more we interacted, the more we could tell she was starting to feel positive about herself. Eventually, she was saying "I'm a runner," as she realized she needed to jump back in the race. The Runner reminded me of an aspect of Ruth: despite the opposition, she persevered, and this woman, through transformation journaling, started running again and was inspired to pick up where she left off and finish each race.

The Artist: Here is a person who had really been hurt and felt uncomfortable. It took her a long time to reveal her name. She resembled Hagar, who had an unexpected encounter with God. She found her voice in her art and recovered it through transformation journaling, which focused her drawing to express how she was feeling. Eventually, she opened up and expressed that she had felt cheated out of life and felt her family was consuming her mind and attention. The Artist was also similar to the woman in the

11. Corbett, *When Helping Hurts*, 53.
12. Corbett, *When Helping Hurts*, 53.

crowd, who had an evolving issue that spread to other areas in her life. In the Artist's case, she had been living a fine life, was middle class, and had a family. To her understanding, a certain person died and then the issue became who would get the house. Unfortunately, the Artist did not get anything from the house, and, like Ruth, she suffered the loss. She was a worker and willing but did not have that critical element of someone extending her opportunities. This is a demonstration to us who would help that being consistent and letting people know we care may lead the suffering eventually to open up and release what has been bottled for so long.

The results of Ruth, Hagar, and the woman in the crowd may differ from those received by the homeless women illustrated above, but their characteristics and experiences (loss, abandonment, loneliness, fear) are similar. The women of the Bible experienced each of these issues but had an encounter that changed their lives forever. That is what we want for the homeless women: that through transformational journaling, they will have an encounter that will change their lives forever. Unlike the women in our biblical text, they depended upon the people of the day to help them in their time of need. The church today can create tools such as transformation journaling to use with homeless women toward the goal of rebuilding their self-esteem based upon a biblical foundation. In this way, we may also rebuild their personalities by sharing God's loving perspective of them, along with God's guidelines for how to live their lives (e.g., free of addiction, not letting themselves be subject to abuse, taking advantage of employment, training, and other positive opportunities).

Even those leading the journaling session can also experience transformation and/or motivation. Although we may be unable to relate to homelessness through personal experience, we can use the journaling prompts to find out where we are or what we need to do. This happened to our leader, Sara Mitchell. Journaling opened the door to taking the sabbatical that had been her goal for quite some time, allowing her to take the steps to become a community chaplain, a goal, we might note, that was first articulated and written down during one of her own journaling sessions. "It might not be transforming," Sara reflected, "but it was certainly motivating."

As for myself, there were many times I went to our weekly women's homeless shelter visit with all intentions of encouraging and lifting them up. While this indeed happened within the community that we built, oftentimes, I left feeling inspired by their testimonies of determination and perseverance.

As Jesus spoke about the poor always being with us (Matt 26:11, Mark 14:7, John 12:8, cf. Deut. 15:11), so always nearby are homeless women and some on the verge of homelessness who are suffering and trying to make it on their own. No one is an island,[13] and as humans, we are created for a relationship: "God designed us for connection with Him and each other."[14] It is always time to help a homeless woman who is lonely, facing many challenges, and really in need of someone who cares. She longs for relationship. and we the church should be the helping hands of Jesus among the homeless, an extension of his *hesed* (lovingkindness, mercy) in the earth: "Social isolation is not always visible—but it's a well-documented fact that a lot of women experiencing homelessness feel alone. Connecting with others in a supportive way is an important aspect of a healthy life—however, it is not always possible when you are living on the street."[15] As the church considers homelessness, let us remember the scripture that mentions how when we receive mercy, we need to give mercy: "Shouldn't you be compelled to be merciful to your fellow servant who asked for mercy?" (Matt 18:33 MSG) This is our way of extending God's hand of mercy to the less fortunate.

Practical ministry among the homeless is important. In her chapter "A Listening Heart," Cathy Squires demonstrates the healing aspects of the community. "She shows how Christians learn from one another and receive healing and support in communities."[16] "We are the salt of the earth" (Matt 5:13–16 NIV). "Salt preserves food from corruption and is necessary to the human diet."[17] Jesus gave the parable recorded in Matthew's gospel that "Jesus' disciples are commanded to preserve the world from general corruption and to shine forth as examples." In this way, "salt and light work together with the Christian community."[18]

Modeling a Biblical Approach to Transformational Journaling

Setting up a journaling program may vary, but here is a practical program for churches, para-church ministries, or a shelter (like a YWCA Shelter,

---

13. Martin, "What's the Meaning of the Phrase 'No Man Is an Island.'"

14. Abell, "Why Do We Prefer Independence over Interdependence," para. 2.

15. Victor, "8 Challenges Homeless Women Face," section 6.

16. DeFazio and Lathrop, *Creative Ways*, xxi.

17. DeFazio and Lathrop, *Creative Ways*, xix.

18. DeFazio and Lathrop, *Creative Ways*, xix.

or Christian halfway houses), where homeless women can explore within these groups some relevant information for understanding themselves and can acquire renovating tools for improving their lives. The transformational journaling motif in my experience is something that has been successful in changing their lives.

The book of Psalms seems to best reflect this motif of journaling.

Although the biblical psalms are not true examples of "journaling," they do illustrate how the truth of our experiences can be expressed alongside the truth of who God is. The varied themes in the Psalms and their unabashed candidness demonstrate how we can be perfectly honest with ourselves and with God about our feelings and thoughts. In journals, we can express ourselves to God and remind ourselves of his greatness. Luke 2:19 tells us about Mary treasuring the events around Jesus' birth and pondering them in her heart. Psalms 111:2 (NIV) says, "Great are the works of the LORD; they are pondered by all who delight in them." Journaling can help us ponder the good things of God and give him praise.[19]

The journaling experience can be the beginning of taking an introspective look, rebuilding the lives of homeless women, their self-esteem, and reflecting on who they are in God's sight as shown through biblical truths.

Why Journaling?

Because of its effectiveness, journaling is often used in recovery programs. It is stated that "journaling, or keeping a regular record of experiences and feelings, especially as they relate to your recovery, can be a helpful tool to advance your healing process."[20] A helpful guide is from one of the books we used for our journaling sessions, *Spiritual Journaling: Recording Your Journey toward God*,[21] which gives sample outlines and provides a structure for journaling. In recent years there has been an uptick in advertising and publishing as it relates to biblical journaling and its effect.

With Bible journaling, you will find a creative and fresh approach to the age-old discipline of Bible reading. With pen in hand, you can visually capture Scripture, meditate on God's word and memorize the text. Some choose to journal as an expression of private devotion, others journal as

19. GotQuestions.org, "What Value Is There in Christian Journaling?" para. 3.

20. Milios, "Journaling as an Aid to Recovery," para. 1.

21. Peace, *Spiritual Journaling Recording Your Journey toward God*.

an act of worship and there are even some who consider it a creative outlet that can be shared.[22]

While journaling is used in recovery, "Bible journaling is an exciting way to engage with Scripture. It can transform the way you spend time in the Word and it all begins within the margins of the Bible,"[23] There are many types and ways of journaling that can be used and may take on several other forms:

- Diary—where you write down the events of the day and how you felt about them.

- An Evening Reflection Journal—where you reflect on the day's events and ponder ways that you may have thought or behaved differently that would have involved making better choices.

- Gratitude Journal—where you write about things that you are grateful for and appreciative of.

- Goal-Focused Journal—where you keep track of your goals and objectives and your progress toward the goals and objectives.[24]

Starting a Transformational Journaling Group

Before beginning a journaling group, it is important to understand what it means and the responsibility of its undertakings. We began the journaling group (Journal of Personal Discovery with Arts and Words) at Woods-Mullen Women's Shelter in Boston, starting out with us surveying the need. This is an important step to get an idea of what they want and might be interested in. We found that in this particular shelter, a church was already providing worship services, so we collectively agreed that a journaling group could bring balance to the lives of the participating women. We outlined a proposal and brief program to the leadership of the intent for our shelter visits. Within that proposal included the purpose, scope of the plan, and advertisement.

22. Magness, "What Is Bible Journaling," para. 2.

23. Magness, "What Is Bible Journaling," para. 1.

24. Milios, Rita "Journaling as an Aid to Recovery," para. 2.

Purpose

This is a faith-based outreach to provide a "space" in which women can discover their strengths and discuss various issues which present barriers to recovery. We purpose to discover God's perspective on these issues and assist these women in being able to thrive in any situation they encounter, while at the same time the women volunteering hope to develop mutually transforming relationships with the women at the shelter.

Scope of Plan

Depending on the size, try and have a group of at least four women who will volunteer to go to the homeless shelter weekly. We found that starting with a pilot program helped us to gauge where we needed to go and make alterations.

Advertisement

Outreach at Woods-Mullen Women's Homeless Shelter

Express Yourself
by *Creating your own*
Journal of Personal discovery
with
Art and Words

Starlight Ministries invites you to a
Journal Workshop
Wednesdays 7:00pm
third floor Activity room

Volunteer Training Preparation

There are some first steps that should be considered before undertaking this type of ministry in terms of information as well as attitudes and behavior.

Make a Commitment

- Meet once a week for the first three weeks of the month at the shelter.

- On the fourth week, meet for a debriefing session with the volunteers. This provides a place for the women volunteers to talk and think about lessons learned and things that were important and life-giving.

- Collectively pray for the requests of the women.

- Also, use this time to bring more structure to the process and make necessary changes for the following weeks.

- Understand how and why people become homeless.

- The impact of repeated losses.

- Crisis of relationships.

- Effects of mental illness, addictions, family dysfunction, domestic abuse.

- Look at the system of Homelessness at EGC.org for the complete Starlight System Diagram and opportunities for churches to engage.[25]

- Obtain knowledge of the population you are planning to engage with and some specific facts.

Twelve Must-Know Facts about Women and Homelessness

1. Among industrial nations, the US has the largest number of homeless women and the highest number on record since the Great Depression.

2. An estimated 50 percent of all homeless people are women.

3. Up to 92 percent of homeless women have experienced severe sexual or physical assault at some point in their lives.

4. 57 percent of homeless women cite sexual or domestic violence as the direct cause of their homelessness.

5. 63 percent have been victims of violence from an intimate partner.

6. 32 percent have been assaulted by their current or most recent partner.

---

25. "Systems and Diagrams."

7. 50 percent of homeless women experience a major depressive episode after becoming homeless.

8. Homeless women have three times the normal rate of post-traumatic stress disorder.

9. Homeless women are twice as likely to have drug and alcohol dependencies.

10. Homeless women between eighteen to forty-four years old are five to thirty-one times more likely to die than women in the general population.

11. Homeless women in their mid-fifties are as physiologically aged as housed women in their seventies.

12. Victims of domestic violence experience major barriers in obtaining and maintaining housing and often return to their abusers because they cannot find long-term housing.[26]

Adopt Appropriate Attitudes and Behaviors

Volunteers need to have factual information and be prepared cognitively, but also in attitude and behavior. Some of which can be summarized in the PLEDGE (below). It is by keeping our attitudes and behaviors in mind that we were able to provide a safe, nurturing "space" where transformation can take place.

You can rehearse this PLEDGE acronym silently, or choose something similar that relates to people experiencing homelessness:

P   Pray your way through every interaction.

L   Listen, be in the non-judgmental zone, don't be shocked.

E   Empathize, be aware of the shame and power dynamics.

D   Decide to be a friend, not a fixer, caseworker, or mother.

G   Give privacy, before and after the encounter, where many issues are involved.

E   Empower, encourage, and validate their story; their situation is not who they are.

26. Stanberry, "12 Must-Know Facts," para. 1.

Sample Journaling Session

The Woods-Mullen journaling group developed this program outline that we used at our journaling sessions that may be helpful to others interested in beginning a program.

Outline

6:15   Arrival time

Announce workshop (over intercom due to women in various places).

Welcoming people is important! So, start with something that allows your group to know what you desire and their expectations. First impressions are lasting impressions. As the slogan says, "You never get a second chance to make a good first impression (Will Rogers)."

> Welcome _____
> to Starlight Ministries Journaling Workshop. Our prayer is to create a safe and non-judgmental space where we all can be open/ honest with ourselves and each other. Journaling is a great way to see growth/ enlightenment and to create worthwhile dialogue. Refraining from derogatory comments and giving unsolicited advice will help maintain a positive and safe atmosphere positivity within the group. Thank you for participating in this workshop.
>
> God Bless.   *Wilma, Ana, Rachelle, Elizabeth and Sara*

6:30   Greeting and general conversation

6:40   Topic introduced and activity for the evening

Since it has been established that journaling is helpful in recovery programs to help individuals heal, we found that biblically based journaling can be transformational and life-giving. Since people express themselves in many ways, we would present topics, relevant Bible passages, and a way to discuss, journal, artistically express, and then respond to the topic or subject matter.

- Provide the women with colored pencils, markers, and decorative elements (stickers) so they can respond to the initial topic either creatively or with words.

- Start with a topic that is relevant, such as "who are you?"

6:45   Writing (individually, with meditation music in the background)

- Women may write, draw, or color their topic responses.

- When they are finished, the women are invited to share their thoughts.

7:15   Open with sharing and discussion

- This leads to further discussion and integration of the biblical element.

- Engage with the women with their questions and concerns.

8:00   Announcements

8:05   Prayer requests

- Allow quiet time and offer the women to share and give prayer requests.

8:15   Closing prayer

8:30   Pack up

Through the exercises in our journaling sessions, women were able to take an introspective look, reflect on who they are in God's sight, and listen to each other, which helped to promote healing, dignity, self-esteem, and their worth as a child of God. As a result, the consciousness of these women was heightened into realizing God loves and values them and his intent is they better their situation to help others better theirs.

Here are statements from some of the women in our journaling sessions:

- "I have a new job and am in training."
- "I am working on patience."
- "Trying to stay on the right path."
- "After 12 years of being crack-free, I started going to church. Being here in tonight's journaling session is making me smile, although it's my son's two-year death anniversary."

- "I learned the sacrifice of God's son that we all have eternal life."
- "I have a change in my understanding of faith, self-confidence, consistency, and helping others."

These statements indicate that women are feeling valued and experiencing real growth, self-understanding, and empowerment, which means they are experiencing transformation.

Exercises That Model a Biblical Approach to Transformational Journaling

The Psalms best reflect this journaling motif reminding us we are not alone in our life's journey.

The lament psalms in particular (e.g., Pss 6, 42, 51) show how it is never wrong to cry out your complaints, sorrow, or loneliness, especially to God. When we release to the right person, things can turn around. If the psalmist in the Bible did, so can we!

The scriptures and reflective questions should arouse your appetite for more of the Psalms.

Psalm 6 (MSG)

Please, God, no more yelling, no more trips to the woodshed. Treat me nice for a change; I'm so starved for affection. Can't you see I'm black and blue, and soul? God, how long will it take for you to let up? Break in, God, and break up this fight; if you love me at all, get me out of here. I'm no good to you dead, am I? I can't sing in your choir if I'm buried in some tomb! I'm tired of all this—so tired. My bed has been floating for forty days and nights On the flood of my tears. My mattress is soaked, soggy with tears. The sockets of my eyes are black holes; nearly blind, I squint and grope. Get out of here, you Devil's crew: at last God has heard my sobs. My requests have all been granted, my prayers are answered. Cowards, my enemies disappear. Disgraced, they turn tail and run.

Reflections

1. Why do you think the psalmist is so honest?

- Are you this honest with God in your prayers? Explain.

- If yes, has being honest caused you to trust God?

- If not, do you feel being honest would help you to trust God?

Being open and honest with God can bring relief to wherever you are troubled. Will you put your trust in God?

Psalm 10 (MSG)

God, are you avoiding me? Where are you when I need you? Full of hot air, the wicked are hot on the trail of the poor. Trip them up, tangle them up in their fine-tuned plots . . .

They mark the luckless, then wait like a hunter in a blind; When the poor wretch wanders too close, they stab him in the back. The hapless fool is kicked to the ground, the unlucky victim is brutally axed. He thinks God has dumped him, he's sure that God is indifferent to his plight. Time to get up, God—get moving. The luckless think they're Godforsaken. They wonder why the wicked scorn God and get away with it, Why the wicked are so cocksure they'll never come up for audit. But you know all about it—the contempt, the abuse. I dare to believe that the luckless will get lucky someday in you. You won't let them down: orphans won't be orphans forever . . . God's grace and order wins; godlessness loses. The victim's faint pulse picks up; the hearts of the hopeless pump red blood as you put your ear to their lips. Orphans get parents, the homeless get homes. The reign of terror is over, the rule of the gang lords is ended.

Reflections

1. Think of a time you felt neglected by everyone, including God. Describe what that was like.

2. When it seems the arrogant are prospering and the less fortunate suffering, what are your thoughts?

3. If God were sitting next to you right now, what is one question you would ask him?

It may seem that God is far away, but he sees, he is just,
and is there to help you. Will you give God a try?

Psalm 42 (MSG)

[1] A white-tailed deer drinks from the creek; I want to drink God, deep draughts of God.

[2] I'm thirsty for God-alive. I wonder, "Will I ever make it—arrive and drink in God's presence?"

[3] I'm on a diet of tears—tears for breakfast, tears for supper. All day long people knock at my door, Pestering, "Where is this God of yours?" [4] These are the things I go over and over, emptying out the pockets of my life . . . [8] Then God promises to love me all day, sing songs all through the night! My life is God's prayer. [9] Sometimes I ask God, my rock-solid God, "Why did you let me down? Why am I walking around in tears, harassed by enemies?" [10] They're out for the kill, these tormentors with their obscenities, Taunting day after day, "Where is this God of yours?" [11] Why are you down in the dumps, dear soul? Why are you crying the blues? Fix my eyes on God—soon I'll be praising again. He puts a smile on my face. He's my God.

Reflections

1. Have you ever been so thirsty that nothing seemed to quench your thirst?

2. What have you tried to just make the thirst go away?

3. Reading this Psalm, have you asked the question "Will I ever make it—arrive and drink in God's presence? What did that conversation sound like?

God is there to satisfy your thirst and make you smile again.
Will you allow him the opportunity?

Conclusion

Wilma Faye Mathis

I BEGAN THIS BOOK IDENTIFYING the problem of homelessness and applying strategies based on scriptural principles as a solution. Why? In Matt 8:20, Jesus describes his itinerant ministry: "Foxes have holes and birds of the air have nests, but the Son of Man has no place to lay his head" (NIV). Why did the God of the universe identify with the homeless? Because God's heart is so full of love and compassion for the destitute that, in Lev 25:35, he commands believers to help them: "If any of your fellow Israelites become poor and are unable to support themselves among you, help them as you would a foreigner and stranger, so they can continue to live among you" (NIV).

What does this say to the postmodern Christian? Jesus lives inside each one of us, we are mandated to help the homeless among us. The number of homeless in the United States has increased since the pandemic. I summarized the situation of the US homeless population providing statistics to define the issue (chapter 1). Christians know God calls them to help the poor, but they don't always know how to do that. I described challenges of the homeless women I mentored in chapter 2 as a guideline that explores biblical foundations to care for their needs. I used Ruth the widowed Moabite in chapter 3 as a parallel to the plight of today's woman with no social status and economic means to survive. Ruth is a good role model for the homeless woman because her devotion to her mother-in-law Naomi and her faith in Yahweh brings her into a good marriage; she bears a son and takes her place in the lineage of Jesus. In chapter 4, I explored Hagar in Genesis who represents the abandoned, rejected, and abused woman. Modern homeless women are regarded as outcasts and many, like Hagar, experience abuse from employers, lose livelihood, and are abandoned to the streets. Hagar encounters God's love in the desert as the one who sees and hears her affliction. In chapter 5, I explored Jesus' ministry among the marginalized. In Luke 4:18, Jesus modeled how to help the sick and disabled who are alienated, outcast, and marginalized. In this account of the hemorrhaging woman, Jesus healed the woman of her blood issue and gave her a sense of dignity. Jesus calls Christians to do as he did: Heal and validate the suffering with the resources he provides. A brief summary of part one of this book (chapter 6) demonstrates that practical strategies based on scriptural principle (Isa 61:1) "set at liberty those who are bound" (NIV).

In the last part of this book, teachers, psychologists, and social workers described effective strategies for those outreaching to the addicted, abused, mentally ill and the homeless. In chapter 7, "Building Christian Community for the Homeless," Jeanne DeFazio described an outreach she organized that brought the homeless into a diverse Christian fellowship. She included stories from people who have been homeless along with accounts from those who help the hurting to encourage others. In chapter 8, "The Hosanna Foundation," Martha Reyes explained how to heal the mentally ill through Christian-based therapy, sharing how her Hosanna Foundation provides free Christian-based therapy for low-income men and women. In chapter 9, I demonstrated how to "Empower[ing] the Practical Lives of Women through Transformational Journaling Exercises." Olga Soler's afterword, "Those without a Home," details the challenge of homelessness and reminds us all that it is our Christian responsibility to help the homeless (Deut 15:1–9 NIV).

My conclusion is that scripturally based principles provide practical solutions to resolve homelessness. Why? Because of God's promise in 3 John 1:2: "Dear friend, I pray that you may enjoy good health and that all may go well with you, even as your soul is getting along well" (NIV).

Afterword

Those without a Home

Olga Soler

O NE OF MY FAVORITES among classic books is *Les Misérables* by Victor
Hugo. This is a story that shows the redemptive difference between
grace and the law. In it we see a teen (Jean Valjean) who wants to save his
family from starvation, imprisoned for years in a penitentiary and forced
to do hard labor for stealing a loaf of bread. Understandably he grows into
a bitter and hardened man who does whatever violence or dirty deed he
needs to do to survive. His family probably died from poverty or disease,
now a distant memory; he is an animal capable of anything. One of the
prison guards (Javert) takes special notice of him for his great strength.
Ever after Javert will be a foil to him. When Jean leaves after serving his
sentence, he is warned by Javert that if he does not comply with the (almost
impossible) requirements of his probation, he will be found and put back in
his prison hell for life. Javert will make sure of this because he is convinced
that "once a criminal, always a criminal."

Jean tries to find work but everywhere he goes, as soon as his papers
are shown, he is profiled and told to move on. No one wants to hire him,
and there are no resources for him to find food or help. He is back where
he started years ago as a youth: rejected, cold, hungry, and without solace.
Then, just as he is giving up, someone kindly directs him to a priest in a
town he was passing. He goes to the home of the priest who invites him
in like a long-lost brother. He feeds him, lets him sleep in a real bed, and
treats him like a human being.

Jean is grateful but he knows this is only for a night, and he knows
what awaits him after. So, he does what comes naturally after a life of
dysfunction and chaos. He notices a set of silver candlesticks and some

silver dishes and cutlery and wakes in the night to steal them. He even hits the priest on the way out.

Later he is captured by the police and returned to the house. "He claims you gave him the silver," says the gendarme. Jean knows it is back to jail for sure now. But the priest surprises him with "I am disappointed in you Jean. You took the dishes but did not take the candle sticks that were the most precious of all." To the police he says, "Yes, I gave him everything. Thank you for doing your jobs, but he is innocent." This act of unmerited grace transforms Jean and the priest tells him: "You no longer belong to evil Jean. With this silver I have purchased your soul. You now belong to God."[1]

I love this story for so many reasons. I know I have been in Jean's place as a sinner that deserves nothing but scorn, and I know I have been helped by beloved people of God and their magnanimous Lord, who gave me enough grace, not just for a day but for a lifetime. You ask what the homeless need, and of course it is a home, but they really need so much more, and with it they can (like Jean) become giants of grace pouring forth more and more blessings into the world. How do I know this? I see it every day. I work with the homeless and it is true.

Ministering to the lowest of the low (as many consider the homeless) is not an easy thing. Of course, as believers, we need to have the heart of Christ on this matter. So the big question is "does Jesus want us to care about the poor and homeless?" After all, he was homeless himself. Is it really such a big deal? To talk to some homeless people, it isn't. They like living free of society's rules and sleeping in places not fit for human habitation. Some choose the lifestyle instead of the rat race. They feel as free as a hitchhiker on the Appalachian trail. Having nothing can be liberating, and many believers, like Francis of Assisi, have taken vows of poverty and are satisfied with it.

Still, others are not blessed this way. They long for home and the comfort of warmth and meals cooked on their own stove, but they have none. There is a word in the Welsh language that has no direct translation in English. The word is "hireth," and it roughly means "a home never attained but greatly desired." Perhaps that home is heaven and to many they will never see it here on earth, but I cannot help feeling that if we help someone get an earthly home who has long been deprived of one, that will do for now; we are doing God's work.

---

1. Hugo, *Les Misérables*, 27–28.

Just because some choose homelessness does not let the church off the hook. The fact is that caring for the poor is a test of discipleship. Matt 25:31–46, or the famous parable of the sheep and the goats, tells us the master's thoughts about helping the needy. Jesus clearly states that what we do for the poor, we do for him, and what we don't do for the poor, we don't do for him. Further, he states that in the end, when the souls of all men are laid bare before the throne, he will not acknowledge those who did not have his compassion for "the least of these." Perhaps we need to check our discipleship standards if we are not doing something for the poor.

There are also many directives in the Torah that ensure help for the poor. In fact, when the poor are cared for it ensures the financial security of the whole nation. God takes this very seriously.

> At the end of every seven years you must cancel debts. [2] This is how it is to be done: Every creditor shall cancel any loan they have made to a fellow Israelite. They shall not require payment from anyone among their own people, because the Lord's time for canceling debts has been proclaimed. [3] You may require payment from a foreigner, but you must cancel any debt your fellow Israelite owes you. [4] However, there need be no poor people among you, for in the land the Lord your God is giving you to possess as your inheritance, he will richly bless you, [5] if only you fully obey the Lord your God and are careful to follow all these commands I am giving you today. [6] For the Lord your God will bless you as he has promised, and you will lend to many nations but will borrow from none. You will rule over many nations but none will rule over you. If anyone is poor among your fellow Israelites in any of the towns of the land the Lord your God is giving you, do not be hardhearted or tightfisted toward them. [8] Rather, be open-handed and freely lend them whatever they need. [9] Be careful not to harbor this wicked thought: "The seventh year, the year for canceling debts, is near," so that you do not show ill will toward the needy among your fellow Israelites and give them nothing. They may then appeal to the Lord against you, and you will be found guilty of sin. (Deut 15:1–9 NIV)

Imagine a country with no poor. This could be such a country because it is among the richest in the world. Still, sadly, there is much poverty. On the other hand, there are such places on the earth with very little poverty (the Isle of Man for instance; I have visited Man and seen this for myself), but they have taken big steps to end poverty there and have nearly succeeded. Also, lest you think this verse gives permission to extort the foreign poor, there are many verses that say that Israel should welcome the stranger and treat the foreigner who lives among them with generosity and difference, not like an outsider. Further, the prophet Isaiah says this:

> Is not this the fast that I have chosen? to loose the bands of wickedness, to undo the heavy burdens, and to let the oppressed go free, and that ye break every yoke? Is it not to deal thy bread to the hungry, and that thou bring the poor that are cast out to thy house? when thou seest the naked, that thou cover him; and that thou hide not thyself from thine own flesh? Then shall thy light break forth as the morning, and thine health shall spring forth speedily: and thy righteousness shall go before thee; the glory of the LORD shall be thy reward. Then shalt thou call, and the LORD shall answer; thou shalt cry, and he shall say, Here I am. If thou take away from the midst of thee the yoke, the putting forth of the finger, and speaking vanity; And if thou draw out thy soul to the hungry, and satisfy the afflicted soul; then shall thy light rise in obscurity, and thy darkness be as the noon day: "And the LORD shall guide thee continually, and satisfy thy soul in drought, and make fat thy bones: and thou shalt be like a watered garden, and like a spring of water, whose waters fail not." (Isa 58:6–11 KJV)

These are amazing promises for the children of God. Still, people will say this is all well and good, but that is the Old Testament. We don't live under that kind of "bondage" anymore. I will refer you back to the sheep and the goats and many other verses in the New Testament that tell us taking care of the poor is our job as the body of Christ. In heaven there will be no poverty, nor will there be wealth. Both things are a byproduct of sin. The things we consider items of wealth will be building materials on par with cement and mortar in the kingdom of God (see the streets of gold and the walls of precious stones of the book of Revelation). Their only attraction will be that they reflect the light of God.

Is God no longer interested in us working on poverty by helping the poor in an effective way? Israel was sent into exile so that "the Land would enjoy her Sabbaths."[2] Which was a direct reference to the Sabbatical cycle that was to ensure no poverty in Israel. Some believers (scholars, laypeople and some who are business savvy) have found interesting correlations between financial disasters and the seven-year cycle of the year of release. It may be that God is not done with the idea of his sovereignty over the land and his passion for the poor just yet.

2. Lev 25:4; 2 Chr 36:21; Jer 25:11.

The homeless need housing, but we might as well say they need the moon in our society, as housing is astronomically expensive. As a counselor who works with the homeless, displaced, mentally ill, ex-cons, and drug addicts in recovery, housing is the worst problem we must face after sobriety. Finding a place to live or a job if you have a "history" is a problem. At the present time, landlords are asking for criminal record checks as well as credit checks (which may even eliminate many upstanding citizens from renting, especially if they have had medical troubles and fallen behind on bills).

When a person works really hard on his or her sobriety, and he or she cannot find work or a place to live, they often fall back on criminal activity as a matter of survival. If there had been no saintly priest to save Jean Valjean, he would no doubt have become a thief again or worse. There are many more obstacles as well to these people during stabilization. In this economic climate and with these handicaps, what hope do the homeless have of getting a place to live that offers real shelter?

A woman at a party once asked me to explain why there are so many homeless in such a rich country. Amazed that she would ask such a question, I was happy to give her what answers I could. Those I pass on to you in this writing. First, however, I would like to know why you think there are so many homeless. Among the answers I have gotten to that question are the following:

"People are lazy and don't want to work."

"People take advantage of the system."

"Who cares why they are homeless, it's not my problem."

"Maybe it's bad karma. They are paying for their sins."

"People are mentally ill and should be in a hospital."

"Poor people are irresponsible and don't deserve the help they get. Why should we help them anymore?"

"The homeless are dope fiends and alcoholics and they have used up all their money on their addiction."

Some of the people that make such comments change their minds as they navigate current options for rentals or home purchases themselves. They discover that rents and mortgages are expensive. So expensive in fact that a person with a good job may find they are spending more than half of their earnings on their rent or mortgage. If they want to live in a safe place with good schools for their children, they must pay even more.

Probing a little, they may also discover that the increase in the cost of rentals and mortgages is still ongoing. Some people, even financially savvy people, are wondering when the increases are going to stop. Many reasons are given for these increases, but the bottom line is that real estate is money and those that have it want to make as much money as they can. There used to be ceilings on rents and mortgages, or laws that said you can charge so much for this kind of property and no more, but there aren't now. Laws that protected people from these often-outrageous increases have been taken away. This benefits people who have, but really hurts those who have less. It kills those who have nothing. So whatever reason is given, the bottom line is that rents are going up because no one is saying they can't, and this is a real problem all over the country. Here is a little radio conversation from Alabama's WBRZ radio that may shed some light on the subject:

> The fallout from soaring rent prices isn't just a headache when looking for a place to live. According to a market analyst, un-affordable rent has financial implications that are extremely detrimental to the quality of life. Nick VinZant with Lending Tree, an online lending marketplace, explained rent prices have been steadily increasing over the last decade, blowing the lid dur-ing the COVID-19 pandemic.
>
> You can't just say to landlords that you have to charge less, and you can't say to people you got to make more money," Nick VinZant with Lending Tree complained." In Alabama, we've seen a 13% increase in the last year; that's unbelievable," VinZ-ant exclaimed. According to rentdata.org, in Jefferson County, a 2-bedroom apartment averaged a little more than $1000 in 2021. The same place would have cost about $873 in 2019. The financial fallout was terrible for the quality of life of residents, according to VinZant." If you are paying more than 30% of your total income on rent, you are considered it to be housing cost-burdened, that's because if you're paying that much it's difficult to afford other household necessities," VinZant said. Alabama is one of the most cost-burdened states in the nation, he said. "What we found when we looked at Alabama is nearly 50% of renters, one out of every two people, are housing cost-burdened," he explained. VinZant said soaring rent prices were a problem elected leaders needed to address because double-digit percent rent increases and 2–3% pay raises was math that did not add up." Fundamental policy changes with elected leaders having

more investment in affordable housing and relaxing zoning laws that would allow affordable housing to be built.[3]

This is of course one expert's take on the problem. There are others. Places like Boston and its surrounding areas see even greater leaps in costs. Alabama is no longer the hardest hit by increases. Seattle has taken the lead and many other cities are in the running.[4] Cities are also where the jobs are. That is quite a dilemma for those who need to work to rent (that would be most of us). Further we see rents doubling or tripling in a maneuver called gentrification.

Now remember we are talking about the homeless, but I want to help you understand that homelessness can happen to just about anyone. A fire or an illness or a downturn in your finances due to some tragedy can bring you to that place especially if you, like most Americans, are living paycheck to paycheck. Even if you have tucked away three months of savings you are still navigating a thin line if your rent or mortgage is over half your income. I've seen people who were ex-public officials and heirs to fortunes living in missions. It's not impossible. What we fail to do for the poor now may be what we must face when we *are* the poor later. It behooves us to fix this now.

Gentrification

Gentrification: what is it and why does my church need to know about it to serve the homeless? Gentrification can hit just about any neighborhood that is not lucrative enough for its landlords. It is a move to turn a poor neighborhood into an upscale area. It can happen practically overnight. In fact they want it to happen quickly so people don't have a chance to get together and challenge it legally. The rents double or triple and if you can't afford it (who can?) you need to leave. When you leave you are on your own resources, which for the poor are very little. Getting housing can take years as HUD housing has long wait lists. I've seen families with children and elderly all displaced in a matter of months.

Of course, there are always two sides to the story. Italics are mine:

> For many, the allure of living in a fast-growing, increasingly af-
> fluent area is an exciting notion (*if you can afford it*). The rise of

3. "Why Rent Prices Are So High," paras. 2–10.
4. "Report: Rental Prices Skyrocket in Seattle," para. 1.

newer real-estate structures, increased business investment in the area, and a plethora of new jobs can create (*for those who can afford to live near there*) an entirely different community atmosphere than the one which previously existed.[5]

Then there is the other side. Those who have no resources or choices in the matter. Those who lose their shelter for someone else's profit. Recommendations can be made even by government agencies, but without regulations, they amount to nothing:

> However, the CDC (Center for Disease Control and Prevention) has some recommended action steps for communities, planners and public health professionals to prevent some of these adverse effects:
>
> 1. *Create affordable housing for all incomes*
>   - Develop mixed-income communities
>   - Adopt inclusionary zoning policies
>   - Identify incentives (e.g., tax breaks and credits) for planners, developers, and local governments to control displacement
> 2. *Approve policies to ensure continued affordability of housing units and the ability of residents to remain in their homes*
>   - Consider code enforcement policies that assist residents with home improvements
>   - Consider implementing rent controls
>   - Preserve federally subsidized housing programs
>   - Consider location-efficient mortgages that provide competitive rates and low down payments to those who want to live in "location-efficient communities" that are convenient to resources and reduce the need to drive
> 3. *Increase individuals' assets to reduce dependence on subsidized housing*
>   - Consider homeownership programs
>   - Explore job creation strategies and programs
> 4. *Ensure that new housing-related investments benefit current residents*

5. "Pros and Cons of Gentrification," para. 1.

- Review development proposals to determine whether the changes could cause displacement

5. *Involve the community*

- Allow the community to provide input into the design and redevelopment of their neighborhoods
- Educate the community on their available options
- Create organized bodies and partnerships that develop programs to mitigate gentrification.

The last item on this list is probably the most important. Involving communities early on, as the signs of gentrification are first beginning to show, is a very crucial piece of the puzzle. Affected communities should feel empowered to prevent displacement and to have a say in how their neighborhood will change. Stabilizing the community economically through a variety of the methods mentioned here is an important step, as well as thinking outside of the box to incorporate alternative forms of home ownership or community ownership to preserve the institutions that are key to social well-being.[6]

Unfortunately, one of the tacit reasons for gentrification is to get rid of what is perceived as the "riff-raff" and to get wealthy people in who will raise the level of wealth in the area. This way all the people who have, will have more. Why would these people actually want to "spend" money on helping those they have just gotten rid of? They don't. Compensations for displacement are few and far between.

Which Poor Deserve Help?

A large part of the consensus, even among believers, is that there are deserving poor and undeserving poor. In my experience working with the poor for over twenty years, most of the poor who are able to work are employed (some have two or three jobs just to make ends meet). Most legally, some "under the table" because they need more to live than minimum wage, and you can't always find work that pays well over the table. If you ask me what percentage of the poor are worthy of assistance and how many are *taking advantage of the system*, I would say the percentage of those taking advantage who are able-bodied (not mentally ill or handicapped, not elderly or

6. "Other Side of Gentrification," para. 1.

children, not illiterate or learning disabled, not sick or traumatized) is very, very small. Memes about the "welfare mom who drives a Cadillac" are put online by people that should sit where I sit every day before they judge. They should also try walking a mile in the shoes of those they criticize. I would say much of this propaganda against the poor is cruel and false.

I must admit that when I hear people talking about the poor and homeless as if they could magically wave a wand and get a good education and a good job and could afford most housing today, I want to cry. Sure, there are people who take advantage of the system. Many of them make six figures or more in pay and have many ways to write off their taxes. By contrast the poor who do take advantage usually impact their own families and take relatively little from the state. In addition, they are often so beaten down they have given up. We all know white-collar crime does far more damage to society than the purse snatchers on the street and the wealthy seldom get blamed for it.[7] When a poor person takes advantage of the system, they are usually so broken a prison cell would be an upgrade. That is why they have stopped trying. This is not an excuse to take drugs and break the law to survive, but these are some of the reasons they do it.

If you want to see the poor who you think are playing the system, take a walk down in the Bowery in NYC or Methadone Mile in Boston. These places with their pathetic inhabitants often look like a scene from *Night of the Living Dead*. Do you really think these people are "getting one over" on the system? Would you like to trade places with them for their welfare money ($300 a month) or their social security check ($1000 a month max, usually more like $750)?

It is Expensive to be Poor

Jesus once stood outside of the temple watching the wealthy toss in their coins for a temple offering. The disciples were impressed, as were the pass-ersby, but Jesus (apparently the only one who could do math in the crowd) was not impressed at all with them. Instead, he praised a widow who tossed in two mites (less than a penny).[8] He knew she gave more than those with money because she gave all she had. If someone who makes $100,000 drops

7. "White-Collar Vs. Blue-Collar Crimes," para. 3.

8. Mark 12:42–44 and Luke 21:1–4.

a thousand in the offering plate, he still has quite a lot of money. If someone who has nothing gives what little they have, the math is pretty clear.

People who are poor, who must spend a third or a half of their income for housing, are taking money away from many other needs. Food, clothing, utilities, transportation, insurance, etc. If what they make is not much, you see the problem. Even with food stamps, which, thank the Lord, are still available in this country, they live with hardship. Then again when they work and declare what they make, the food stamps are reduced significantly, so there we are. There are so many other ways the poor pay more. Yet you will see them sharing what they have on a regular basis.

When I went to seminary in Boston, I didn't know anyone. I would walk the streets after school to get to the subway and I would feel the loneliness all around me. Then I started to work at the Boston Rescue Mission. The street people from all over town would come to the mission every night to get some food from the soup kitchen there. I got to be known as one of the mission ladies, and soon everywhere I went in Boston I met "friends" who waved and smiled at me. They would escort me through dangerous areas just to make sure I was safe.

Street people are not shy about their gratitude, and though they often had scuffles when they were drunk or high, they also had a remarkable culture of sharing. One woman finally achieved the "holy grail" of Section 8 housing and left the mission homeless for a snug little apartment. She was strictly warned not to live with visitors. After a while however, she got so lonely, she started coming back to the soup kitchen every night just to be with her friends. The homeless have feelings. They really do.

On that note I will say for those who want a home or have had one and lost it, the feelings are hard to manage at times and substance abuse becomes part of survival for them. It helps them forget. If you really want to delve into their psyche, you might want to read anything by Gabor Maté, a doctor out of Vancouver, Canada. He can also be found on YouTube in various eye-opening videos.[9] Gabor has really captured their ethos and their pain and talks about the fact that most people who live in the street have had terrible trauma. The stories are heart-wrenching. For their pain alone I am glad to be one of those who cares for them. Mental illness, bad luck, and severe emotional and physical pain is often their lot. The disorientation is real and the despair is palpable.

9. Maté, Gabor. "Power of Addiction."

A young male who ended up in my office because of homelessness and alcohol dependency told me this when I asked him the question "What is a nice, smart, middle-class white kid like you doing in a place like this?" He said,

> Despair leads you to strange places. I had a good home but I started drinking because I could not manage the anxiety I lived with. The drink was all I thought about after a while because it would help me, but I lost everything to it. Yet despair was not enough to give me the strength to go forward. When you are in the street, priorities get mixed up. Booze became more important as an anesthetic than a place to stay. One day melted into the next and months went by. It was kind of liberating in a way not to be tied to the clock. Unless you have been there it's hard to know what it's like. Not having a home sort of steals your brain when you are out there.

I love it when people talk about all that "scum" that get welfare checks and live in government housing. Would you like to live on what they have? Would you like to live where they do? If you had a choice, would you? Do you have any idea how long it takes them to get a dingy little place in a HUD housing or Section 8 apartment? Most HUD housing has a wait list of ten to fifteen, and Section 8 is the same. And when you get to the promised land of HUD or Section 8, what is waiting for you? Is it luxurious? You will be happy if it keeps the cold out on a January day, but it may not keep the bugs and mice out.

Then again, where do people go as they wait? They used to live with a friend or relative, but now landlords can say no one is allowed to live in a place but those on the lease. So where do they go? If you have a car you live in a car. (Lots of kids and parents live in cars these days.) If you can't do that, you may live in a shelter, sleeping on a cot by night and leaving to find your "fortune" during the day. There are wait lists for shelters too. If you can't find shelter you may live in a tent in a city park or the woods (all year long). You may live in a sleeping bag under a bench or in an alley. You may steal something so you can get arrested and at least have three square meals and a warm cell.

The system of housing itself makes us crazy. You may go ten years on the waitlist, and if your name comes up and you don't have a mailing address (even if they have your government cell phone number), if they can't send you a letter somewhere and you don't respond right away, you lose your place. I've seen people go near suicidal over losing a place they waited on for ten to fifteen years. So many are waiting because housing for the poor is limited. They have lost so much housing to gentrification. Minimum wages can't keep up with regular housing. Education and training is expensive. The agencies have lots of people apply. They can't afford to wait for a person that has no mailing address. If you don't keep them posted they drop you, but as we have seen homelessness is disorienting. One forgets things that are not part of immediate daily survival.

Many Other Reasons for Homelessness

Do you think you could ever be homeless? What would it take? How about sickness and the cost of insurance and medical care? When you are down on your luck and you have to downgrade your medical insurance, you also have to downgrade your care. If a middle-class person finds it frustrating to get an appointment with a doctor these days, just imagine a doctor at a local clinic who has up to four thousand patients. (I called one not too long ago). How long will a patient have to wait to see his doctor if they have four thousand patients? Heaven help that person if she has a serious illness. But we are talking about homelessness, right? So, when you have a serious illness, and you can't work because you are sick, and you have to wait months to see a doctor, how long will it take for you to lose your job and not be able to pay your rent? Then how long will it take for you to be homeless? I have read articles by professionals that have fallen prey to illness and found themselves without shelter because of this very scenario. How long would it take you to become poor if you got really sick? Not long.

How about if you are a victim of abuse and you have nowhere to run and few resources? It happens every day. This is the reason some spouses stay home and take the abuse. There are shelters for the abused, but that puts you on long housing wait lists unless you can get a very good job that can help you afford a regular apartment. You need first, last, and security to get into an apartment. That can get pricey. The welfare may help but again, there are long lists, and money runs out for such programs. If you are a victim of abuse, you need to find a hole somewhere and start stashing away any money you can. That is no joke.

Single parents are also in trouble when it comes to finding housing. One income and children to support is difficult. In the present housing milieux it's twice as hard unless you make good money or have family help. Moving in with another single parent in similar trouble may be the answer. If you have good friends or family, this is the time to stick together. If you don't, heaven help you.

In general, if you want to know why rents are skyrocketing (and they are) there are many reasons and none of them are good. We are in a housing crisis and greed and deregulation has a lot to do with it, but we are hoping things will turn soon. They have to or we may all be in trouble. If you want to read more about it, I recommend an article by Catherine Smith of the *Huffington Post*.[10] There are also some good books out there about it. It would also be important for you to understand that this is a real crisis exacerbated by things like recessions and pandemics. All of us will be impacted. We have to help each other. Divided, we may not have the resources we need to move forward. The forces that are dividing people today and leading them to seek their own welfare over that of others will cost them when they are out there alone themselves.

Could we be homeless someday? It's possible. Many poor people believe. God takes care of us, but things happen, and we may see some serious things before it's all over. Should we help the homeless now? Yes. Should we learn to help each other? Yes. God uses people to accomplish his ends.

So What Can the Church Do?

So, what can we as the church do to make things better? We can go countercultural. If we are landlords, we can charge less for rent. We know we will still make money. We can make sure our rentals have everything they need to do well. Yes, we can still be firm about damage and put responsibility where it belongs, but we don't have to be hard-nosed about it.

If we are a church body looking to help the housing situation, then use the gifts of those in the church. There may be some builders in the congregation that can join with the rest to fund and build structures that will accommodate the poor. Reasonable rent can be charged. Buildings can be purchased and renovated as sober houses or houses for the poor. You can also purchase buildings or groups of apartments for sale. Some people particularly like to sell to non-profit organizations like churches. You can create recovery centers or villages that your church can oversee and help.

Those in the congregation who work for human services like me can give some of their time and find others who will volunteer time to "case

10. Smith, "3 Reasons."

manage" people who live there. They may need guidance. They may need other resources. They may need communication skills or sobriety skills, medical needs, budget training etc. They will need to learn to get along as a community, have community meetings. Maybe even staff a day care for the working parents. Many homeless know more about community than a lot of churches do but still facilitate mutual help and places to have community life. There are people in the church that can help with everything a place like that would need. Firm rules must be in place. We can require sobriety on pain of eviction. We can also have zero tolerance for violence. We can do Bible studies and have worship services in these places for those who wish to attend.

Another option is to adopt local shelters and help them help the people who live there. They may need toiletries or food. They may need direction and pastoral help. They may need a friend who will listen and be there for them. They may need clothes to stay warm. They may need a job. They may need a place to take a hot shower. They may need a ride to services or medical appointments. With good boundaries a church can be essential to local missions already in place. Toys for the kids at Christmas are nice, but they will not help if they have no home to play with them in. Finding them homes should always be a goal. You might even have them to the church for holiday lunch or dinner. What a witness. We could be the hands and feet of Jesus in a very direct way.

You can also be careful who you vote for. We need to demand that something be done about the rising prices of housing because soon we will be the homeless and the poor. Many people who have gotten ill have lost everything to medical costs. It's not impossible for such a terrible scenario to happen. The medical system here in the US needs lots of adjustments to be fair to everyone, especially the poor. Right now, it's kind of "all about the money," not about the health of human beings. If we could tend to our health without going broke, we might have less homelessness, addiction and other terrible things.

Brother Curtis Almquist, SSJE, explains: "We have right now the opportunity to make changes in how we live and share life together. How shall we begin?"[11]

---

11. Almquist, "Making Meaning," 10.

About the Authors

Julia C. Davis has an EdM from the Harvard Graduate School of Education and an EdM from Bouve College of Health Sciences at Northeastern University. She has held teaching certificates in New York, Massachusetts, and the District of Columbia and has been certified as an assistant principal and as an assistant special education supervisor. Julia has taught in the public and private sector in community-based programs including METCO, Summer STEP, opportunities for underrepresented populations in science and technology, and Head Start. She has served as a member of Parent's Advocacy Group for Massachusetts supporting free appropriate public education (FAPE) and mainstreaming special education students. She has taught Pre-K through all twelve grades, adult non-readers, limited English language learners and GED preparation courses. Julia taught internationally as an undergraduate exchange student in a Special Education Program based in Newnham on Severn, Gloucestershire, England, which operated under the auspices of Antioch College in Ohio. Julia and her husband Dan have three children and three grandchildren. They attend the International Family Church in North Reading, Massachusetts.

Jeanne DeFazio is a former SAG/AFTRA (Screen Actors Guild/American Federation of Television and Radio Artists) actress of Spanish-Italian descent, who played supporting parts in theater, movies, and television series, then served the marginalized in the drama of real life. She became a teacher of second language–learner children in the barrios of San Diego. She completed a BA in history at the University of California, Davis, an MAR in theology at Gordon-Conwell Theological Seminary, and the Cal State TEACH English language learners program. From 2009 to the present, she has served as an Athanasian Teaching Scholar at Gordon-Conwell's multi-cultural Boston Center for Urban Ministerial Education.

Wilma Faye Mathis holds a Doctorate, an MDiv, an MA in Urban Ministry, and a graduate certificate in Christian studies. Rev. Dr. Mathis has served the church as Christian education director, hospitality president, and national women's department vice president. She is a desktop publishing entrepreneur and now works as a Senior Project Manager at a community health center in Boston, while she conducts her own community ministry to homeless women and her own personal ministry to moms and other women (Mom2Mom Ministry: "a place where someone cares"). Additionally, Wilma hosts inductive Bible studies, an expansion to her ministry, called Biblical Learning Center (BLC). She also serves as an Athanasian teaching scholar in Dr. William David Spencer's systematic theology courses at Gordon-Conwell Theological Seminary, Boston Campus (CUME).

Dr. Martha Reyes was born in Puerto Rico and has resided in California, ministering to Hispanics in the United States and internationally since 1978. She has traveled to more than twenty-two Latin American countries and many parts of Europe and the Middle East, giving concerts and retreats on inner healing and participating as a guest speaker in national and international conventions on healing and restoration. From 1992 until the year 2000 she organized the acclaimed Hosanna Multi-Festivals conventions, international events with representatives from thirty countries in music, theater, and arts, held annually in Mexico, Florida, and Israel.

Olga Soler is a director, writer, and performer for Estuary Ministries, a Christ-centered performing arts ministry dealing with biblical themes, inner healing, abuse, and addiction problems. The art forms used include drama, dance, storytelling, mime, comedy, graphic arts, writing, film, and song. Olga attended the High School of Performing Arts (as seen in the movie *Fame*), the Lee Strasberg Theatre and Film Institute, and the Herbert Berghof Studio in New York City. She has performed widely at conferences, churches, prisons, coffee houses, support groups, youth groups, and retreats and has even performed on the streets, at secular colleges, and in worship services across the United States and the United Kingdom. She holds degrees in education and communications with equivalent studies in theology and psychology. She studied for two years at Gordon-Conwell Theological Seminary. She has designed and conducted the workshops

"Dance Alive" and "Trauma Drama" at many Christian recovery conferences. She wrote the curriculum for and conducted discovery groups for addicts at the Boston Rescue Mission, using the arts to help them process aspects of their recovery. She also conducts workshops for Christian drama and dance in many churches of all denominations. Using Paulo Freire's *Pedagogy of the Oppressed*, she wrote a script for the Mosaics group of parents, helping their children, who were victims of sexual abuse, through the court system and assisting them in filming the script for a documentary. She performed and coauthored scripts for four years with the Christian ministry named Team in Massachusetts and conducted eight full-scale multimedia presentations out of the Rio Ondo Arts Place in Woburn, Massachusetts, including *Voice of the Martyrs*, *Techno Easter*, and *Clean Comedy Night*. She has directed and choreographed entire productions at universities and colleges, including *A Man for All Seasons*, *Jane Eyre*, *Amal and the Night Visitors*, and (by permission of the author) Calvin Miller's *The Singer*. She wrote and illustrated the book *Epistle to the Magadalenes* and has conducted retreats for women using the book accompanied by dramatic presentation. She is the author of many other books and assorted screenplays. She is the proud mother of three wonderful children, Cielo, Reva, and Ransom. She lives in Massachusetts with her husband, Chris, and her Japanese Chin dog, Kiji. Email: fleursavag@yahoo.com.

Bibliography

"The 2017 Annual Homeless Assessment Report (AHAR) to Congress." U.S. Department of Housing and Urban Development, Dec 1, 2017. https://www.novoco.com/sites/default/files/atoms/files/hud_2017_ahar_p1_120617.pdf.

"The 2018 Annual Homeless Assessment Report (AHAR) to Congress." Dec 1, 2018. https://www.wpr.org/sites/default/files/2018-ahar-part-1-compressed.pdf.

Abell, Sarah. "Why Do We Prefer Independence over Interdependence? It's Making Us All Sad." *Christian Today*, Sep 7, 2014. https://www.christiantoday.com/article/why-do-we-prefer-independence-over-interdependence-its-making-us-all-sad/40321.htm.

"About Friends." Friends of Boston's Homeless. https://fobh.org/about-fobh/.

Abrams, Mark. "'Homeless Jesus' Sculpture Now on Display in Philadelphia." *CBS Philly*, Jul 31, 2017. https://philadelphia.cbslocal.com/2017/07/31/homeless-jesus-sculpture-now-on-display-in-philadelphia/.

Absher, Jim. "Female Veterans Are Fastest Growing Segment of Homeless Veteran Population." *Military.com*, Mar 28, 2018. https://www.military.com/militaryadvantage/2018/03/28/female-veterans-are-fastest-growing-segment-homeless-veterans.html.

"Addressing Chronic Homelessness: What the Research Tells Us." National Alliance to End Homelessness, Jan 9, 2019. https://endhomelessness.org/addressing-chronic-homelessness-research-tells-us/.

Alexander, David, et al. *Eerdmans Handbook to the Bible*. Grand Rapids: Eerdmans, 1992.

Almquist, Curtis. "Making Meaning." *Cowley* 47.1 (Fall 2020). https://issuu.com/ssje/docs/2020_cowley_fall___pages.

Bal, Mieke. *Death and Dissymmetry: The Politics of Coherence in the Book of Judges*. Chicago: University of Chicago Press, 1997.

Barry, John D., ed. *The Lexham Bible Dictionary*. Bellingham, WA: Lexham, 2015. Logos.

"Basic Facts on Homelessness in Massachusetts and Across the Country." Massachusetts Coalition for the Homeless. https://www.mahomeless.org/about-us/basic-facts.

Bauer, Walter Wilbur, et al. *A Greek-English Lexicon of the New Testament and Other Early Christian Literature*. 3rd ed. Chicago: University of Chicago Press, 2000.

Bedford, Tori. "'I Have No Place to Go': City Evicts and Arrests at Mass and Cass, Clears Tents." *GBH News*, Nov 2, 2021. https://www.wgbh.org/news/local-news/2021/11/01/i-have-no-place-to-go-hundreds-leave-mass-and-cass-as-city-clears-tents.

"Beyond Stigma and Stereotypes: What Is Homelessness?" Anti-Defamation League. https://www.adl.org/sites/default/files/beyond-stigma-and-stereotypes-what-is-homelessness.pdf.

Blacketer, Raymond A. "Book Review: Writing the Wrongs: Women of the Old Testament among Biblical Commentators from Philo through the Reformation." https://www.academia.edu/30983746/Book_Review_Writing_the_Wrongs_Women_of_the_Old_Testament_among_Biblical_Commentators_from_Philo_through_the_Reformation.

Bock, Darrell L. *Luke 1:1–9:50*. Baker Exegetical Commentary on the New Testament 1. Grand Rapids: Baker Academic, 1994.

———. *Luke*. The IVP New Testament Commentary Series. Downers Grove: InterVarsity, 1994.

"Boston's 'Methadone Mile' and the Wars on Drug Users, Unhoused People." *Filter*, Feb 18, 2021. https://filtermag.org/bostons-methadone-mile-and-the-wars-on-drug-users-unhoused-people/.

Bouma-Prediger, Steven, and Brian J. Walsh. *Beyond Homelessness: Christian Faith in a Culture of Displacement*. Grand Rapids: Eerdmans, 2008.

Brandt, Brad, and Eric Kress. *God in Everyday Life: The Book of Ruth for Expositors and Biblical Counselors*. The Woodlands, TX: Kress Christian, 2007. Logos.

Broll, Ryan, and Laura Huey. "'Every Time I Try to Get Out, I Get Pushed Back': The Role of Violent Victimization in Women's Experience of Multiple Episodes of Homelessness." *Journal of Interpersonal Violence*, 35.17–18 (May 19, 2017). http://journals.sagepub.com/doi/abs/10.1177/0886260517708405.

Bromiley, Geoffrey W., and James A Patch. "Gleaning." In *The International Standard Bible Encyclopedia*. Grand Rapids: Eerdmans, 1995. https://biblehub.com/topical/g/gleaning.htm.

Brown, Francis, et al. *The Enhanced Brown-Driver-Briggs Hebrew and English Lexicon*. Oak Harbor, WA: Logos Research Systems, 1977.

Brown, Jerry. "We Have to Restore Power to the Family, to the Neighborhood, and the Community with a Non-Market Principle, a Principle of Equality, of Charity, of Let's-Take-Care-of-One-Another. That's the Creative Challenge." https://www.inspiringquotes.us/quotes/BhYI_kgBl8KAR.

Brueggemann, Walter. *Genesis*. Interpretation: A Bible Commentary for Teaching and Preaching. Atlanta: John Knox, 1982.

Brueggemann, Walter, et al. *To Act Justly, Love Tenderly, Walk Humbly: An Agenda for Ministers*. Eugene, OR: Wipf & Stock, 1997.

Butler, Trent C. *Holman Bible Dictionary*. Nashville: Holman Bible, 1991.

Cambridge Greek Testament. Cambridge: Cambridge University Press, 2012.

Chavalas, Mark. "The Comparative Use of Ancient Near Eastern Texts in the Study of the Hebrew Bible." *Research Gate* 5.5 (May 2011). https://www.researchgate.net/publication/261538428_The_Comparative_Use_of_Ancient_Near_Eastern_Texts_in_the_Study_of_the_Hebrew_Bible.

Choge Kerama, Emily J. "Introducing Ruth." In *NIV God's Justice: The Holy Bible: The Flourishing of Creation & The Destruction of Evil*. Grand Rapids, MI: Zondervan, 2016.

Clarke, Adam. *Adam Clarke's Commentary on the Whole Bible: Matthew through Luke*. Vol. 5A. GraceWorks Multimedia, 2011. Kindle ed.

Collins, Adela Yarbro, and Harold W. Attridge. *Mark: A Commentary*. Minneapolis: Fortress, 2007.

Collins, Gerald O. "Jesus and the Homeless." *Thinking Faith*, Feb 3, 2011. https://www.thinkingfaith.org/articles/20110203_1.htm.

Corbett, Steve. *When Helping Hurts: How to Alleviate Poverty without Hurting the Poor . . . and Yourself*. Chicago: Moody, 2014.

DeFazio, Jeanne C., ed. *Finding a Better Way*. Eugene, OR: Wipf & Stock, 2021.

———, ed. *The Commission: The God Who Calls Us to Be a Voice During a Pandemic, Wildfires, and Racial Violence*. Eugene, OR: Wipf & Stock, 2021.

DeFazio, Jeanne C., and John P. Lathrop, eds. *Creative Ways to Build Christian Community*. Eugene, OR: Wipf & Stock, 2013.

DeFazio, Jeanne C., and William David Spencer, eds. *Redeeming the Screens*. House of Prisca and Aquila Series. Eugene, OR: Wipf & Stock, 2016.

DeFazio, John Joseph. *Specialist Fourth Class John Joseph DeFazio: Advocating for the Disabled American Veterans*. House of Prisca and Aquila Series. Eugene, OR: Wipf & Stock, 2020.

DiFazio, Joe. "Long Island a 'Big Piece' of How Boston Plans to Fight Opioid Crisis." *Patriot Ledger*, Jan 10, 2022. https://www.patriotledger.com/story/news/2022/01/05/new-boston-mayor-weighs-potential-uses-long-island-quincy-bridge/9087829002/.

Dillon, Amanda. "Bible Journaling as a Spiritual Aid in Addiction Recovery." Multidisciplinary Digital Publishing Institute, Nov 3, 2021. https://www.mdpi.com/2077-1444/12/11/965.

Dionne, Brittany. "Why Rent Prices Are So High and What Can Be Done about It." *WBRC*, Feb 28, 2022. https://www.wbrc.com/2022/03/01/why-rent-prices-are-so-high-what-can-be-done-about-it/.

"Domestic Violence and Homelessness." National Coalition for the Homeless. https://www.nationalhomeless.org/publications/facts/domestic.html.

Dozeman, Thomas B. "The Wilderness and Salvation History in the Hagar Story." *Journal of Biblical Literature* 117.1 (1998) 23–43. https://doi.org/10.2307/3266390.

Dreier, Peter. "Poverty in America 50 Years after Michael Harrington's *The Other America*." *Huffington Post*, Mar 25, 2012. https://www.huffingtonpost.com/peter-dreier/post_3167_b_1378516.html.

Drey, Philip R. "The Role of Hagar in Genesis 16." Andrews University Seminary Studies. Andrews University Press, 2002. https://www.andrews.edu/library/car/cardigital/Periodicals/AUSS/2002-2/2002-2-04.pdf.

Dupere, Katie. "7 Unique Challenges Homeless Women Face—and What You Can Do to Help." *Mashable*, Apr 13, 2016. https://mashable.com/2016/04/13/homeless-women-challenges/.

Easton, Matthew G. *Illustrated Bible Dictionary and Treasury of Biblical History, Biography, Geography, Doctrine, and Literature*. New York: Harper, 1893.

Edwards, James R. "Markan Sandwiches the Significance of Interpolations in Markan Narratives." Brill. Jan 1, 1989. https://doi.org/10.1163/156853689X00207.

Ehrenreich, Barbara. *Nickel and Dimed: On (Not) Getting By in America*. New York: Metropolitan, 2001.

Eichstedt, Judy. "Give Me Shelter." *ProQuest* 122 (2014) 48–51. https://search.proquest.com/docview/1722618238?accountid=173955.

Elwell, Walter A., et al. *Baker Encyclopedia of the Bible*. Vol. 2. Grand Rapids: Baker, 1988.

"Emergency Shelter." Boston Public Health Commission, Feb 19, 2021. https://www.boston.gov/government/cabinets/boston-public-health-commission/homeless-services/emergency-shelter.

"Emergency Shelter." FamilyAid. https://familyaidboston.org/our-work/emergency-shelter-v2/.

Emmanuel Gospel Center. https://www.egc.org/.

Eusebius. *Eusebius—the Church History: A New Translation with Commentary.* Translated by Paul L. Maier. Grand Rapids: Kregel, 1999.

"Facts about Homelessness 2022." Backpack Bed. https://backpackbed.org/us/facts-about-being-homeless?gclid=Cj0KCQjwlK-WBhDjARIsAO2sErSQ31J9nW69B5lQP27_OVv5JFIy7eu-0-YBMekl7PGwUosRExbI4PgaAobyEALw_wcB.

"Family Homelessness." Mass Law Reform Institute, Jul 10, 2018. https://www.mlri.org/advocacy-issue/family-homelessness-2/.

Fensham, F. Charles. "Widow, Orphan, and the Poor in Ancient Near Eastern Legal and Wisdom Literature." *Journal of Near Eastern Studies* 21.2 (Apr 1, 1962) 129–39. https://www.jstor.org/stable/543887?read-now=1&seq=1#page_scan_tab_contents.

Fewell, Danna Nolan. *The Children of Israel: Reading the Bible for the Sake of Our Children.* Nashville: Abingdon, 2003.

Finley, M. I. *The Ancient Economy.* Berkeley: University of California Press, 1999.

Freedman, David Noel. *Anchor Bible Dictionary. Vol. 3, H-J.* New York: Doubleday, 1992.

Freedman, David Noel, et al. *Eerdmans Dictionary of the Bible.* Grand Rapids: Eerdmans, 2000.

Freeman, James M., and Harold J. Chadwick. *Manners and Customs of the Bible.* New Kensington, PA: Whitaker, 1996.

"Frequently Asked Questions." National Health Care for the Homeless Council. https://nhchc.org/understanding-homelessness/faq/.

Funkhouser, Mark. "What People Get Wrong about 'Political Will.'" *Governing.* Apr 23, 2021. https://www.governing.com/gov-institute/on-leadership/gov-political-will-lbj.html.

Gardiner, Alan Henderson. *Egypt of the Pharaohs.* Oxford: Oxford University Press, 1966.

Gardner, Julie. *Original Voices: Homeless and Formerly Homeless Women's Writings.* Seattle: Mary's Place, 2016.

Garnsey, Peter, and Richard P. Saller. *The Roman Empire: Economy, Society and Culture.* Oakland: University of California Press, 2015.

Glatz, Carol. "Pope Francis: Concern for Poor Is Sign of Gospel, Not Red Flag of Communism." *National Catholic Reporter,* Jun 16, 2015. https://www.ncronline.org/blogs/francis-chronicles/pope-francis-concern-poor-sign-gospel-not-red-flag-communism.

Guzik, David. "Study Guide for Ruth 1." *Blue Letter Bible.* https://www.blueletterbible.org/Comm/guzik_david/StudyGuide_Rth/Rth_1.cfm.

"Hagar." *New World Encyclopedia.* https://www.newworldencyclopedia.org/entry/hagar.

Hampson, Margaret Daphne. *Theology and Feminism.* Oxford: Blackwell, 1991.

Harper, Robert Francis. *The Code of Hammurabi, King of Babylon.* Chicago: University of Chicago Press, 1904. https://oll.libertyfund.org/title/hammurabi-the-code-of-hammurabi#Harper_0762_391.

Harrington, Michael. *The Other America: Poverty in the United States.* Baltimore: Penguin, 1971.

Harris, R. Laird, et al. *Theological Wordbook of the Old Testament*. Chicago: Moody, 2004. Logos.

Henry, Matthew. *Matthew Henry Study Bible: King James Version*. Edited by A. Kenneth Abraham. Peabody, MA: Hendrickson Bibles, 2010.

Hiebert, Paula S. "The Biblical Widow." In *Gender and Difference in Ancient Israel*, edited by Peggy L. Day. Minneapolis: Fortress, 1989.

Hoffmeier, James Karl. *Israel in Egypt: The Evidence for the Authenticity of the Exodus Tradition*. New York: Oxford University Press, 1999.

Holladay, William L. *A Concise Hebrew and Aramaic Lexicon of the Old Testament*. Grand Rapids: Eerdmans, 2010. Logos.

Holy Bible: English Standard Version. Wheaton, IL: Crossway Bibles, 2001.

"Homelessness and Addiction." Addiction Center. https://www.addictioncenter.com/addiction/homelessness/.

"Homelessness in America: Focus on Families with Children." United States Interagency Council on Homelessness. https://www.usich.gov/resources/uploads/asset_library/Homeslessness_in_America_Families_with_Children.pdf.

"Homelessness Questions & Answers." The Homeless Hub. https://www.homelesshub.ca/resource/homelessness-questions-answers.

"How Many People Experience Homelessness?" National Coalition for the Homeless. http://www.nationalhomeless.org/publications/facts/How_Many.pdf.

"How Many Shelter Beds Are Enough?" *Open Minds*, Nov 19, 2018. https://www.openminds.com/market-intelligence/executive-briefings/how-many-shelter-beds-are-enough/.

Hugo, Victor. *Les Miserables*. https://freeclassicebooks.com/Victor%20Hugo/Les%20Miserables.pdf.

Hurley, James B. *Man and Woman in Biblical Perspective*. Eugene, OR: Wipf & Stock, 2002.

James, Carolyn Custis. *The Gospel of Ruth: Loving God Enough to Break the Rules*. Grand Rapids: Zondervan, 2008.

James, Carolyn Custis, and Craig G. Barthomoew. *Finding God in the Margins: The Book of Ruth*. Bellingham, WA: Lexham, 2018.

Johnston, Katie. "As Chelsea Begins to Blossom, Struggles Remain." *Boston Globe*, Jan 15, 2016. https://www.bostonglobe.com/business/2016/01/15/chelsea-booms-poverty-drugs-persist-square/vLjfjRxUcziZB9XFS5p1OP/story.html.

Jolicoeur, Lynn. "This Doctor Has Spent Decades Treating Boston's Homeless Population and Says City's Tent Crisis Is Worst He's Seen." *WBUR*, Oct 29, 2021. https://www.wbur.org/news/2021/10/29/boston-homeless-mass-and-cass-tent-encampment.

Kitchen, K. A. *Ancient Orient and Old Testament*. London: InterVarsity, 1966.

Kittel, Gerhard, and Geoffrey Bromiley, eds. "Widow." In *Theological Dictionary of the New Testament*. Vol VI. Grand Rapids: Eerdmans, 2006.

Kleven, Alyssa. "Report: Rental Prices Skyrocket in Seattle." *MYNorthwest*, Dec 26, 2012. https://mynorthwest.com/8001/report-rental-prices-skyrocket-in-seattle/.

Kuruvilla, Abraham. *Genesis: A Theological Commentary for Preachers*. Eugene, OR: Resource, 2014.

"A Lack of Services for Homeless Women and Families." United Women in Faith. https://harborumw.nccumc.net/files/2016/01/A-Lack-of-Services-for-Homeless-Women-and-Families.pdf.

Lamb, Anna. "Wu Says Tents Will Be Cleared from Mass & Cass by Jan. 12." *Bay State Banner*, Dec 22, 2021. https://www.baystatebanner.com/2021/12/15/wu-says-tents-will-be-cleared-from-mass-cass-by-jan-12/.

Lamerson, Samuel. *The Graeco-Roman Background of the New Testament in Faithlife Study Bible*. Bellingham, WA: 2016. Logos.

Lapide, Cornelius à, and Thomas Wimberley Mossman. *The Great Commentary of Cornelius à Lapide*. Edinburgh: John Grant, 1908.

Liddell, Henry George, and Robert Scott. *Greek-English Lexicon*. Salt Lake City: Genealogical Society of Utah, 2009.

Linthicum, Robert C. *Empowering the Poor*. Monrovia, CA: MARC, 1996.

"Local Church Assistance Programs for Veterans." http://freegrantsforveterans.org/local-church-assistance-programs-for-veterans/

Lockyer, Herbert. *Women of the Bible: The Life and Times of Every Woman of the Bible*. Grand Rapids: Lamplighter, 1995. Kindle.

Louw, J. P., and E. A. Nida. *Greek-English Lexicon of the New Testament: Based on Semantic Domains*. Vol. 1. New York: United Bible Societies, 1996.

Magness, Nathan. "What Is Bible Journaling?" *Lifeway*, Feb 26, 2016. https://www.lifeway.com/en/articles/bible-journaling-for-beginners.

Magnum, Douglas, et al. *Genesis 12–50*. Lexham Research Commentary. Bellingham, WA: Lexham, n.d. Logos.

"Mark." In *Women's Bible Commentary*. Edited by Carol A. Newsom and Sharon H. Ringe, 267. Louisville: Westminster John Knox, 1998.

"Mark 5:25-26—Exposition." *Bible Portal*. https://bibleportal.com/commentary/section/pulpit/690843

Marshall, I. Howard. *The Gospel of Luke*. The New International Greek Commentary. Grand Rapids: Eerdmans, 2017.

Martin, Gary. "What's the Meaning of the Phrase 'No Man Is an Island?'" *Phrase Finder*. https://www.phrases.org.uk/meanings/no-man-is-an-island.html.

Maté, Gabor. "The Power of Addiction and the Addiction of Power: Gabor Maté at TEDxRio+20." YouTube, Oct 9, 2012, 18:46. https://www.youtube.com/watch?v=66cYcSak6nE.

Mathis, Wilma Faye. "Jesus Among The Homeless." Fort Knox Seminary Doctoral Dissertation. 2022. Unpublished.

Maynark, Jill, ed. *Reader's Digest Illustrated Dictionary of Bible Life and Times*. New York: Reader's Digest Association, 1997.

McKiernan, Kathleen. "Advocates Worry Homeless Pupils' Lives 'Are Being Ignored' in Crisis." *Boston Herald*, Nov 18, 2018. https://www.bostonherald.com/2016/08/15/advocates-worry-homeless-pupils-lives-are-being-ignored-in-crisis/.

McKiernan, Kathleen. "Special Report: Nearly 4,000 Students Homeless as Boston Crisis Deepens." *Boston Herald*, Nov 18, 2018. https://www.bostonherald.com/2016/08/15/special-report-nearly-4000-students-homeless-as-boston-crisis-deepens/.

Mel Novak Official Website. March/April 2022 newsletter. http://melnovak.com/wp-content/uploads/2022/05/Mar-Apr-2022.pdf.

Milios, Rita. "Journaling as an Aid to Recovery." *Recovery.org*, Dec 13, 2021. https://recovery.org/pro/articles/journaling-as-an-aid-to-recovery/.

"Mind/Body Connection: How Emotions Affect Health." *Familydoctor.org*, April 18, 2022. https://familydoctor.org/mindbody-connection-how-your-emotions-affect-your-health/.

New American Standard Bible. La Habra, CA: Lockman Foundation, 1995.

NIV Archaeological Study Bible: An Illustrated Walk through Biblical History and Culture. Grand Rapids: Zondervan, 2005.

Olivet, Jeff. "4 Simple Ways to End Homelessness." *Huffington Post,* Feb 15, 2017. https://www.huffingtonpost.com/entry/4-simple-ways-to-end-homelessness_us_58a45fe9e4b08obf74f04294.

"The Other Side of Gentrification: Health Effects of Displacement." International Making Cities Livable. https://livablecities.org/2013/04/11/blog-other-side-gentrification-health-effects-displacement/.

Owen, Brit. "HUD Report Finds Overall Drop in Homeless Last Year." *RISMedia,* Feb 7, 2022. https://www.rismedia.com/2022/02/07/hud-drop-homless-2021/.

Packer, J. I., et al., eds. *ESV Global Study Bible: English Standard Version.* Wheaton, IL: Crossway, 2012. Logos.

Patterson, Richard D. "The Widow, Orphan, and the Poor in the Old Testament and Extra-Bibilical Literature." *Bibliotheca Sacra* (Jul 1973) 223–34. https://nanopdf.com/download/the-widow-orphan-gordon-college-faculty_pdf.

Peace, Richard. *Spiritual Journaling: Recording Your Journey toward God.* Colorado Springs: NavPress, 1998.

Peecook, Emily. "Hagar: An African American Lens." *Denison Journal of Religion* 2 (2002) https://digitalcommons.denison.edu/cgi/viewcontent.cgi?article=1023&context=religion.

Perkins. "Widow." In *Baker Encyclopedia of the Bible* 2. Grand Rapids: Baker, 1988.

Piper, John. "Christ in Combat: Offense by the Spirit." *Desiring God,* Mar 25, 1984. https://www.desiringgod.org/messages/christ-in-combat-offense-by-the-spirit.

"Policy and Advocacy - Melnea Cass / Mass. Ave. 2.0." City of Boston, Jun 7, 2022. https://www.boston.gov/government/cabinets/boston-public-health-commission/mass-and-cass-showing-whats-possible.

"Poverty." Homeless Hub. https://www.homelesshub.ca/about-homelessness/health/poverty-0.

Powell, Mark Allan. *The HarperCollins Bible Dictionary.* San Francisco: HarperOne, 2011.

"The Pros and Cons of Gentrification." *MReport,* Jan 23, 2017. https://themreport.com/daily-dose/01-23-2017/pros-cons-gentrification.

Reader's Digest Illustrated Dictionary of Bible Life and Times. New York: Reader's Digest Association, 1997.

Reiling, J., and J. L. Swellengrebel. *A Handbook on the Gospel of Luke.* New York: United Bible Societies, 1993.

Rengstorf, Karl Heinrich. "Διδάσκω." In *Theological Dictionary of the New Testament,* edited by Gerhard Kittel and Gerhard Friedrich. Vol. 2. Grand Rapids: Eerdmans, 1977. Logos.

"Safe Havens." HUD Exchange. https://files.hudexchange.info/resources/documents/SafeHavens.pdf.

Smith, Catharine. "3 Reasons Why Your Rent Is So High." Jun 26, 2019, https://www.huffpost.com/entry/high-rent-reasons_n_5do3d65ae4b0304a120f25e4.

Spencer, Aida B., and William David, eds. *Christian Egalitarian Leadership: Empowering the Whole Church According to the Scriptures.* Eugene, OR: Wipf & Stock, 2020.

Stanberry, Joanna. "12 Must-Know Facts about Women and Homelessness." Project Renewal, Mar 13, 2014. https://www.projectrenewal.org/blog/2014/3/13/12-must-know-facts-about-women-and-homelessness.

"Starlight Ministries." Emmanuel Gospel Center. https://www.egc.org/homeless-outreach-learn-more/.

Stickel, Matt. "A Hidden Side of Homelessness: Why Women Avoid Homeless Shelters." Springs Rescue Mission, Oct 5, 2018. https://www.springsrescuemission.org/a-hidden-side-of-homelessness-why-women-avoid-homeless-shelters/.

Stiles, Wayne. "God Will Give You a New Name." Nov 19, 2017. https://waynestiles.com/god-will-give-you-a-new-name.

"Substance Abuse and Homelessness." National Coalition for the Homeless. https://www.nationalhomeless.org/factsheets/addiction.pdf.

Swanson, James. *A Dictionary of Biblical Languages: Hebrew (Old Testament)*. Oak Harbor, WA: Logos Research Systems, 1997.

"Systems and Diagrams." Starlight Ministries https://static1.squarespace.com/static/57ff1c7ae58c62d6f84ba841/t/597f5994e58c621d069cf68e/1501518230589/SL+System+Diagram+v-9.pdf.

Taylor, Emily. "Sculptor Timothy Schmalz on the Story behind His 'Homeless Jesus.'" NUVO, Nov 9, 2016. https://www.nuvo.net/arts/visual_arts/sculptor-timothy-schmalz-on-the-story-behind-his-homeless-jesus/.

"Teresa of Ávila." Wikipedia, s.v. https://en.wikipedia.org/w/index.php?title=Teresa_of_%C3%81vila&oldid=822639554.

Thompson, John Lee. *Writing the Wrongs: Women of the Old Testament among Biblical Commentators from Philo through the Reformation*. New York: Oxford University Press, 2001.

Thurston, Bonnie Bowman. *The Widows: A Women's Ministry in the Early Church*. Minneapolis: Fortress, 1989.

Toombs, L. E. "Clean and Unclean." In *The Interpreter's Dictionary of the Bible*, edited by George Arthur Buttrick. Nashville: Abingdon, 1962.

Trible, Phyllis. *Texts of Terror: Literary-Feminist Readings of Biblical Narratives*. Philadelphia: Fortress, 1984.

"Unique Challenges of Women Experiencing Homelessness." Career and Recovery Resources, Inc. https://www.careerandrecovery.org/unique-challenges-of-women-experiencing-homelessness/.

Wallis, Jim. *God's Politics: Why the Right Gets It Wrong and the Left Doesn't Get It*. London: HarperOne, 2009.

Western, Dan. "29 Inspirational Mother Teresa Quotes about Giving." *Wealthy Gorilla*. https://wealthygorilla.com/mother-teresa-quotes/.

"What Value Is There in Christian Journaling?" *GotQuestions*. https://www.gotquestions.org/Christian-journaling.html.

"White-Collar Vs. Blue-Collar Crimes: It's Nothing Like You'd Think." *Opinion Front*. https://opinionfront.com/white-collar-vs-blue-collar-crimes#:~:text=It%20is%20evident%20that%20white-collar%20crimes%20involve%20meticulous,been%20a%20role%20reversal%20in%20this%20domain%20too.

"Who We Are." Rosie's Place. https://www.rosiesplace.org/who-we-are.

"Why Are People Homeless?" Pine Street Inn. https://www.pinestreetinn.org/homeless_awareness_month.

"Why We're Here." Rosie's Place. https://www.rosiesplace.org/who-we-are/why-were-here.

Wigoder, Geoffrey. *The Illustrated Dictionary and Concordance of the Bible*. New York: Sterling, 2005.

Wiles, Sunshine. "U.S. Sen. Rockefeller Delivers Farewell Speech." *MetroNews*, Dec 4, 2014. https://wvmetronews.com/2014/12/04/u-s-senator-jay-rockefeller-delivers-farewell-speech-on-capitol-hill.

Williams, Delores S. *Sisters in the Wilderness: the Challenge of Womanist God-Talk*. Maryknoll, NY: Orbis, 2013.

Wilson, William. *Wilson's Old Testament Word Studies*. Peabody, MA: Hendrickson, 1989.

"Women in the Bible: What We Learn from the Book of Luke." Zondervan Academic, Jan 10, 2019. https://zondervanacademic.com/blog/women-bible.

"Woods Mullen Shelter and Services." Homeless Shelters Directory. https://www.homelessshelterdirectory.org/cgi-bin/id/shelter.cgi?shelter=8600.

Victor, Fred. "8 Challenges Homeless Women Face Every Day." Mar 3, 2022. https://www.fredvictor.org/2020/03/03/lets-help-homeless-women.

Voth, Steven. "What's the Good News? Good News of Jesus." *Christianity Today*, Aug 8, 2017. https://www.christianitytoday.com/ct/2000/february7/47.51.html.

Yancey, Philip. *Jesus I Never Knew*. Grand Rapids: Zondervan, 2002.

Young, Robert. *Young's Literal Translation*. Oak Harbor, WA: Logos Research Systems, 1997.